Mastering WordPress And Elementor

A Definitive Guide to Building Custom Websites Using WordPress and Elementor Plugin

KONRAD
CHRISTOPHER

Copyright

Konrad Christopher
ISBN: 9798689056012
ChurchGate Publishing House
USA | UK | Canada
© Churchgate Publishing House 2020

While the advice and information in this book are believed to be true and accurate at the date of publication, neither the authors nor the editors nor the publisher can accept any legal responsibility for any errors or omissions that may be made. The publisher makes no warranty, express or implied, with respect to the material contained herein.

Printed on acid-free paper.

Printed in the United States of America
© 2020 by Konrad Christopher

Table of Contents

CHAPTER ONE

OVERVIEW OF WORDPRESS

In 2020, building websites with zero knowledge of coding has never been easy without WordPress. Business owners, companies and other big organizations - who are not ready to go through the rigor of learning coding and programming only because they want to create a simple website to host their services – use WordPress to create simple and amazing websites, which solves their needs. Literally, WordPress is a free and open source system for managing content built on PHP and MySQL. WordPress, the largest open source content management system (CMS) has become the most used content management system all over the world, which has been noted to power about 32% of the top 10 million websites available online. WordPress began in 2003 as a small and simple blogging platform but has, today, grown into a fully-fledged content management system; all thanks to the multitude of widgets, plugins and themes.

If you are looking for a simple platform that can allow beginners and professionals create and host a simple website, it is WordPress. The WordPress allows you to create your website with simple drag and drop features. All that you need to do is install WordPress on your computer and start enjoying its features to bring your website to live.

Installing WordPress on your computer

Most of the times, you will be able to start your WordPress website by creating a free WordPress account on their website at www.WordPress.com or you can install WordPress on your computer so that you will be able to test and deploy all the features of WordPress locally and then deploy them to create your website. A popular local environment for installing the WordPress is the **WAMP.**

Why install WordPress with WAMP?

- You will get familiar with the WordPress platform and get to know all the basics.
- Test your sites before taking it live.
- Have proper idea of WordPress and experiment with new plugins and features

In this guide, you will be creating WordPress locally with WAMP and at the same time learn how to create a WordPress website that is accessible by the public (live website). Remember that the WAMP server is meant for creating WordPress websites that you can use to experiment and learn how to use various WordPress features. The website you created using the WAMP server is only available locally on your computer and won't be made available live. To create a live website, we will be going through a **domain name** and **web hosting.**

Installing WordPress on Windows using WAMP

There are two common CPU architectures on Windows, which include the 32 bits and the 64 bits Windows architecture. Downloading a WAMP server for local WordPress installation requires choosing between the 32 bits and the 64 bits CPU architecture. In essence, you will need to confirm whether your computer is running on 32 bits or 64 bits before you visit the website where you can download the WAMP file for installation. To check your Windows specification, you can consider the guide below;

- From your computer, you can go (utilize the Window search box at the bottom left of your screen) to the **control panel** and tap on **system and security > system > view amount of RAM and processor speed.**
- You will see a screen that looks exactly like the one above. The CPU architecture for the Window above is 64 bits.
- Now, you can proceed to https://www.wampserver. com/ with any web browser on your computer where you will be able to download and install the WAMP file.
- Once the website has loaded successfully, you will see a page asking you to choose between installing 64 bits and 32 bits WAMP server. Select the WAMP you want to download based on the Window architecture you are running on your computer. The screenshot below is choosing the Window 64 bits version.

- The https://sourceforge.net/projects/wampserver/ also provides a good platform for downloading and installing the WAMP execution file.
- The WAMP server execution file is a bit large (about 518MB). Upon successful file download, simply click on the file to begin the installation process.

- Upon successful installation, you can then proceed to set up a database for your local WordPress.
- To set up your WordPress database, launch the installed WAMP and you will notice a green WAMP icon at the bottom right hand side of the computer screen. If the WAMP server is bringing red or yellow, it is indicative that the apache files that constitute the WAMP are not working efficiently and you are required to restart these services by clicking on their respective icons.

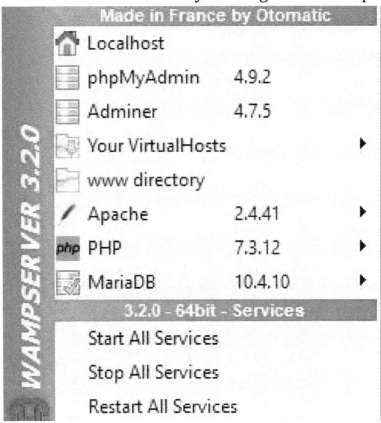

- Launching the WAMP file will show the screenshot above where you are expected to click on the **phpMyAdmin**. Tapping on the **phpMyAdmin** will take you to the **phpMyAdmin** login page on your web browser. The **phpMyAdmin** is a platform where you will be able to manage the **MySQL** database.
- Once the **phpMyAdmin** login page comes up, enter your username as **root** and do not enter anything in the password box (leave it blank). See the screenshot below;

4

Welcome to phpMyAdmin

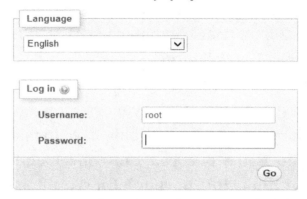

- Once you enter the username **(root)** and password **(blank),** click on the **Go** link below the screen and you will be directed to the phpMyAdmin page. Create a new database for your WordPress website by clicking on the **"databases"** link at the top of the page (see the image below). Input a name for the database (use a name you can remember easily) and write the name somewhere since you will need it later. Tap on the **create** link to create your database. The name of the database created here is **myweb.**

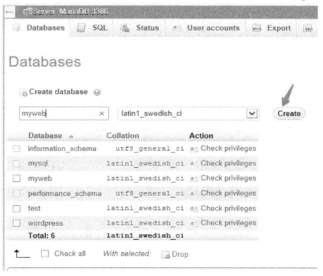

- From your web browser, navigate to the WordPress website at www.wordpress.org to download the latest version of the WordPress as a zip file. Simply click on the **"get icon"** at the top section of the website page to download the latest WordPress version. The latest WordPress version as of September 16, 2020 is the WordPress version 5.5.1 which is the WordPress version you will be coming across more often.

- Extract the downloaded WordPress folder and then copy the folder.
- Go to the location on your computer where you installed the WAMP folder. Usually inside the **C: //Wamp64.**
- Paste the copied WordPress folder inside the **www folder** of the WordPress folder. For easy remembrance, you can rename the copied folder into whatever name you deem fit. You only have to make sure that the name you are changing to is the one you can conveniently remember because the name will serve as the URL of your local WordPress website.
- From the previous images, the WordPress folder was renamed as "**myweb,**" hence you need to navigate to your web browser and enter the address www.localhost/myweb. You will be asked to choose a language after which you will be shown a window displaying the database information. Read and understand the database information and click on the "**let's go**" button at the bottom to continue.

- You will be taken to another window where you will be asked to input the details of your database. Input **root** as the username and leave the password as blank. You will also be asked to input the database username (you were asked in the previous step to note this username).

Below you should enter your database connection details. If you're not sure about these, contact your host.

Database Name	wordpress	The name of the database you want to use with WordPress.
Username	root	Your database username.
Password	password	Your database password.
Database Host	localhost	You should be able to get this info from your web host, if localhost doesn't work.
Table Prefix	wp_	If you want to run multiple WordPress installations in a single database, change this.

Submit

- Once you have input all the necessary information, hit the **Submit button** and WordPress will create your WordPress configuration file in the backend.
- You will be prompted with the "**Run the installation,**" tap the "**Run the installation**" link to continue.
- You will be taken to the WordPress Welcome screen where you will be asked to add a title for your WordPress website. Enter the Admin username, password and the Admin email.
- Click on the **Install WordPress** icon to complete the installation.
- Click on the **Login icon** to go to your **WordPress dashboard**.

Step-by-step guide to getting your website live

To build a WordPress website that will be optimized for search engines and made available to the public, you don't need the WAMP installation procedures. To take your WordPress website live, you should be ready to obtain;

- **A domain name which will used as the name of your website**
- **Web hosting for anchoring your website online.**

7

This section will talk about the steps you will take to register your domain name successfully and almost for free.

A domain name: Is it necessary?

Every day, millions of users and people of all sorts have one or two things to read and purchase online. Let us say, for instance you own a store where you sell shoes and clothes and you wish to have an online platform where buyers can remotely buy your wares and pay without necessarily coming to your store. A simple and quick solution to this is that you can create an e-commerce website from WordPress and then make it available online. The **domain name** for your website is the address where your website is being hosted online. People will be able to enter your website address on their computer to access the information on the website. Without the domain name, accessing your website might seem difficult or almost impossible. This is why you must invest in a good domain name. In summary, the domain name is your website address.

When can you register your domain name?

Since it has been shown that the domain name is your website address, it is important that you register the domain name as soon as a website or a business idea comes to mind. This is partly because another person might take the name if you are not fast enough; and two different websites cannot have the same web address. More often than not, people obtain a domain name before they even create their WordPress account. This is to show you how important a domain name is.

How much should you prepare for the domain name?

Buying a domain name is not something you need to sell your property like most people think. In fact, you can get your domain name for as low as 15 USD. A **.com** domain name is good because it is very common and easily remembered. Most web visitors are more familiar with a **.com** domain name than any other domain name. There are many other domain extensions that you can select from when you are ready to buy one for your website.

Tips to choose the best domain name

You don't just buy a domain name for the sake of it. The domain name, as we have already ascertained, is your website identity on the internet; and as such should not be ambiguous for the purpose of clarity. If it is too ambiguous, visitors will be discouraged and that could mean low patronage for your website or business. Consider the tips below while choosing a domain name for your website;

- Do not use any ambiguous letters, hyphens, ampersands, and numbers in the domain name. This is so that your website can be easily remembered by visitors. Make the domain name simple as much as possible.
- Do not use a domain name that might be considered too long. Let the domain name convey the essence of your website.
- Consider **.com** extension over any other as it is most common and easily remembered by visitors.

How to register your domain name and take your web live

You can buy your domain name with a web hosting from **Bluehost**. Consider the steps below to get the right domain name for your website;

- Go to www.Bluehost.com to select a good plan for your domain name and web hosting. Click on the "**get started**" link at the bottom of the page.

By tapping on the "**get started**" link, you will be directed to the pricing card page where you will be allowed to select your choice. The price of each package will be boldly inscribed.

- Click on the "**select**" link to select a plan.
- You will be taken to a new window where you can either create a new domain name for your website or input an existing domain name or even select a domain name later.

- The "**create a new domain**" menu will allow you to pick any domain extension from the list.

- After tapping **"Next,"** you will be taken to a new window where you can enter some information especially your account information, business name and some other details. Enter your active email address, as they will forward your payment receipt to the provided email address.
- Once you have successfully entered all the necessary information, tap the "**agree to bluehost terms and conditions**" link at the bottom of the page and then choose **"Submit"**
- Upon successful completion of your payment, you will be mailed with detailed instructions on how you can access your web hosting control panel (cPanel). The cPanel provides a platform for easy installation of WordPress.

Installing WordPress from THE cPanel of your web Hosting Dashboard

- From the control panel, scroll to the website section and tap on the **WordPress icon.**
- You will be taken to the Bluehost Marketplace Quick install screen. From this screen, simply click on the **Get started to continue** icon.
- You will be taken to a window asking you to choose the domain name. Pick the right domain name from the drop-down and then tap "**Next**" to proceed.
- Once you tap "**Next,**" you will get a window asking you to input your desired name for the website, Admin username and password for the website. Tap on the "**Install button**" to install your WordPress.

- o Once the installation has been completed, you will get a success message at the top of the page telling you of the successful installation.
- o Click on the "**Installation complete link**" so that you will be taken to the page containing your WordPress login address and password. You should save your username and password somewhere in case you forget. Your WordPress login address will look like http://www.yourdomain.com/wp-admin. Substitute the "your domain" name in this address with the domain name you bought from Bluehost.
- o You can then proceed to login to the WordPress dashboard with your admin username and password.

The image below displays how the WordPress dashboard will look like upon login;

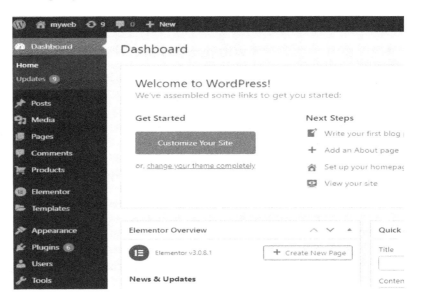

A Tour of the WordPress Dashboard

The WordPress dashboard is what you see once you login to the WordPress account with your username and password. The main essence of logging in to the WordPress dashboard is to access the basic functionalities involved in creating a functioning WordPress website using all the drag and drop menus of the WordPress. Literally, anything you do inside the WordPress account will be reflected on the WordPress live website. A look at the top area of your dashboard will show the name of your website or blog. The "**Howdy, Admin" is** at the top right side of the WordPress dashboard. A tap on the "**Howdy, Admin " will** take you to **Admin, edit my profile and logout** where you can edit some personal information like names, profile picture and then set a new password. Upon successful login to your WordPress, the WordPress dashboard will appear. The dashboard is the powerhouse of WordPress where you can get to see and explore all the features of WordPress. At the top section of your dashboard, you will see the name of your website or blog. Located at the top right section of the WordPress dashboard is the **Howdy, Admin.** When you tap the "**Howdy, Admin,**" you will get access to **Admin, edit my profile and logout.** Each of these three tabs has their functions.

- Tap on the **admin tab** in the image above to add more information about yourself as the owner of the website. Below the **admin** page, there is the **admin color scheme** where you can choose how you want the admin page to look like in terms of color. Tap on each color scheme and you will see the admin dashboard changing based on the color you are selecting. You can also disable the visual editor when writing by tapping on the "**disable the visual editor when writing**" checkbox. Tap on the "**enable keyboard shortcut for comment moderation**" checkbox to enable keyboard shortcuts for users while making comments on website posts. You can also scroll down to the **Name section** on the **admin tab** to enter your names appropriately. The name you input here will replace the "**admin**" in the "**Howdy, Admin.**" Here, Richard Deb is used as the username. Tap on the

"**Display name publicly as**" to select how you want the name to show on the dashboard.

- Tap on the **Update profile** located at the bottom of the screen to update the Admin name and other required information.
- Refresh the dashboard to update the display name. The display name will be updated to Richard and you will see **"Howdy, Richard"** just like it is below;

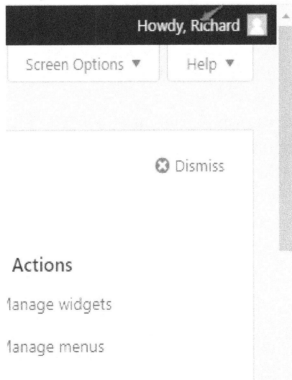

- The *Edit my profile tab* located at the bottom of the **admin tab** contains the same menus as the *Admin tab*.

- Tapping on the **Logout tab** will completely log you out of your WordPress dashboard. Be sure you want to log out before you select this option.

Below the "**Howdy, Richard**" tab contains two other tabs which include; **screen options and the Help tab.** When you click on the **screen options** dropdown, you will see something that looks like the image below;

You can uncheck each of the boxes to remove the information pertaining to the box from the dashboard. For example, un-checking the "welcome" box will remove the welcome page below the dashboard. Un-checking the "Elementor overview" box will remove the information about Elementor from the dashboard.

The **Help** tab contains support and some information you will see on your live website once it has been activated.

Navigating through the WordPress Dashboard

The main navigation bar for your WordPress is located at the left navigation pane of your WordPress dashboard. The WordPress navigation pane contains all the important tabs necessary to activate all settings and updates on your website. There are other features embedded in each menu and you can access them by tapping on each of the menu on the dashboard. The dashboard menus on the left navigation pane are as shown below;

- **Post:** You can leverage the post section to set how your new blog post will appear, post tags and update categories section.
- **Media:** All of the documents, images or files that you uploaded on your blog are stored here. You will be able to explore your media library and edit necessary files.

- **Pages:** This is where to create and have access to all of your pages on WordPress. You will be able to create and maintain WordPress pages here.
- **Comments:** Manage all of your blog comments within this section. Offensive comments can be marked as spam while beneficial comments can be applauded and responded to.
- **Appearance:** In this section, you will be able to manage and see how your website looks. You can choose a new theme, manage widgets for your website and even edit the theme files for your website. You can choose a new theme or edit the themes for your WordPress website.
- **Plugins:** This section provides a platform where you can search and download plugins for your WordPress website. Plugins improve and extend website functionality. For instance, let us assume that you want to create an e-commerce website for your store. You can activate the woo-commerce from the plugins section by searching for and activating the woo-commerce. You can as well insert and delete plugins from this section.
- **Users:** Access all the current users on your website, add new users and delete a user from this section.
- **Tools:** Here, you will be able to manage many sites' convenience tools such as importing and exporting data into and out of WordPress. You will also be able to manage and explore health checks for your website, which gives you the idea of which item on your WordPress requires updating.
- **Settings:** Here, you can configure the name of your website and the URL. You can also set where you want your post to appear on your website and whether people will be able to comment on posts or not. Most of the time, you won't need to change anything under this section once your website has been set up perfectly.
- Tap on the **collapse menu** at the bottom to hide all the menus discussed above from the WordPress dashboard.

The WordPress Toolbar

The Toolbar can be leveraged to access some of the most used WordPress features. To get the toolbar, click on your website's name at the top section of your

WordPress dashboard to enter your live website. From the toolbar, you will have access to the features and functions below;

- Bringing your website's dashboard allowing you access to some commonly used features to update themes, menus and widgets for your website.
- Give you access to the customizer that you can use to update various settings for your website, update your website background and the images in your header.
- See and edit your website comments.
- Add a new user, media, post or page.
- Search any item on your site.
- Manage and edit information on your profile. You will also be able to log out of WordPress from the Toolbar section.

Hiding the Toolbar Section

To hide the **Toolbar section,** follow the steps below;

- From the WordPress dashboard, scroll down and click on **User** in the left navigation pane.
- You will be prompted with the list of users on your site, tap on your own username (admin) or hover your mouse on your username and then tap on the **edit** link beneath your name. Alternatively, click on the "**Profile**" tab beneath the **user** tab on the dashboard.
- You will be taken to your profile page from where you can scroll down and un-select the "**Show Toolbar when viewing site**" box

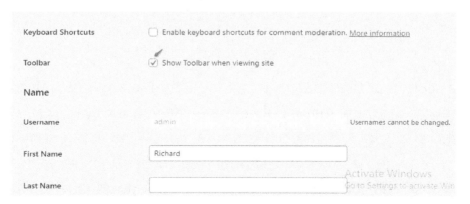

If you want to continue displaying the Toolbar at the top section of your website, select the **Show *Toolbar when viewing site*.**

Posts and pages

WordPress websites are designed around two basic features; **posts and pages.** Posts are blog entries on your blog, which you update as frequently as possible. Posts can include articles on your blog or some personal information you update frequently on your website. **Pages** are used to display content that is not updated frequently on a blog website. A typical example of a page is the "**About us**" page on your blog. You don't usually see the "**about us**" page for a company's website changing that frequently.

To access and check how many posts you have updated on your blog website, simply click on the **Post** menu from the WordPress dashboard. You can always see the following information on the post section; **the author of the post, the category of the post, post's tag, the title of the post, number of comments on your post, the date the post was published or the date of last modification.**

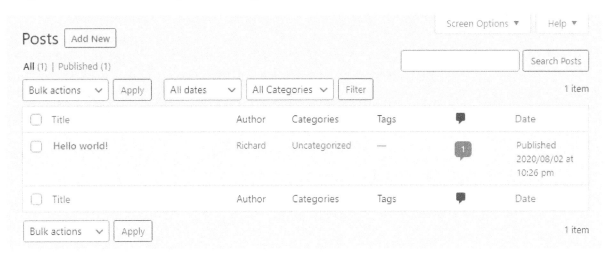

From the top section of the **Post,** you can view how many posts in total you have made on your website, how many published posts you have, your scheduled posts, pending posts, sticky posts, draft posts and posts you have sent to the trash. However, in the image above, you cannot see most of these menus at the top because the website has no scheduled posts nor draft posts currently.

When you hover your mouse over each item on the row, you will see the following menus;

- **Edit:** Tap on this link if you wish to make some editing to that particular post.
- **Quick edit:** Tap on this link to edit some details about the post.
- **Trash:** Click on this menu to delete (trash) that particular post. You can delete all trashed posts permanently when you emptied the trash.
- **View:** Tapping on this will show your post. You will see **preview** instead, if the post has not been published (made available to the public) yet.

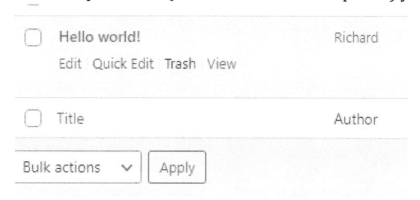

Each post title has a checkbox that will allow you to perform some special actions on multiple items at once. Click on the post that you want to make changes to and select the **Edit menu** or **Move to trash menu** from the **Bulk action dropdown.** Select the **Apply button** to start initiating the changes. The **Edit menu** can be leveraged to make changes to author, tags, categories, status, choose whether to enable comments and pings on your post and confirm whether the posts are sticky or not. The **Move to trash menu** will send the selected item to the trash. You can apply filters to pages with the **Filter button** from the dropdown.

Tapping on the **Screen option** located at the top right section of the screen, which allows you to modify how your post list is being displayed. The **List view** will show your post in the list view format while the **Excerpt view** will allow you to show a brief excerpt of your post beneath the post title. Click on the **Apply icon** to save all the changes you have made.

Page

When you select the **page** menu from the dashboard, you will be able to see the list of pages contained in your blog post. You will get the following details on the page menu; title of the page, the page author, number of comments and the date you publish or last modified the page. See the image below;

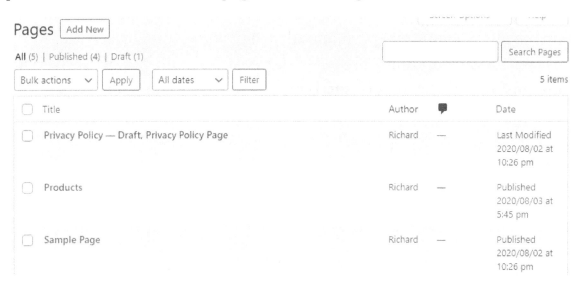

From the top section of the **Page,** you can view how many pages in total you have made on your website, how many published posts you have and your draft pages.

When you hover your mouse over each item on the row, you will see the following menus;

- **Edit:** Tap on this link if you wish to make some editing to that particular page.
- **Quick edit:** Tap on this link to edit some details about the page.
- **Trash:** Click on this menu to delete (trash) that particular page. You can delete all trashed pages permanently when you emptied the trash.
- **View:** Tapping on this will show your page. You will see **preview** instead if the page has not been published (made available to the public) yet.

Each page title has a checkbox that will allow you to perform some special actions on multiple items at once. Click on the page that you want to make changes to and select the **Edit menu** or **Move to trash menu** from the **Bulk action dropdown.** Select the **Apply button** to start initiating the changes. The **Edit menu** can be leveraged to make changes to author, templates, parents, choose whether to enable comments and pings on your pages and check the condition of each of the checked items. The **Move to trash menu** will send the selected item to the trash. You can apply filters to pages with the **Filter button** from the dropdown.

The WordPress Block Editor: Adding Contents on Your Website

In 2018, WordPress released a new text editor called the **Gutenberg editor (Block editor)** alongside WordPress **5.0.** The TinyMCE WordPress editor (**Classic Editor)** was replaced with the drag-and-drop **Block Editor** which gives an improved text editing experience over the **Classic Editor.** With the **Block Editor,** users of various experience levels - with zero knowledge of coding and without having to use any third party plugins and tools – can create custom posts and pages. With the **Block Editor,** you will be able to rearrange, insert and improve your contents with styles while allowing you to add **tables, images, videos, paragraphs, quotes, social media embed and a lot of widgets** to your blog posts. Essentially, the **Block Editor** will allow you to add anything you can imagine to your blog post with a simple drag and drop.

How is the block editor different from the old classic editor?

For the sake of this guide, the **block editor** will be used instead of the **Classic Editor.** Here are the reasons for the preferential choice of the **Block Editor;**

- The new **Block Editor** looks more elegant and polished and utilizes a block system for creating contents.

- **Add tables:** You can easily add tables in your texts without the need to install any additional plugins.
- **Arrange and rearrange your texts while mingling them with text and media** just by dragging and dropping elements from one place to another.
- **Easily create content columns**
- **Change the font sizes and background colors** in each block;

- **Save time by reusing blocks** you have previously used over and over.

How to Add a New Page in the Block Editor

- From the left navigation pane of the WordPress dashboard, scroll to the **Page** tab.
- Click on **Add new page** you will be taken to the section where you will be able to add a new page to your WordPress.

- Click on the "+" icon at the bottom of the "**Add title**" box and you see some list of options to choose from. See the image attached below;

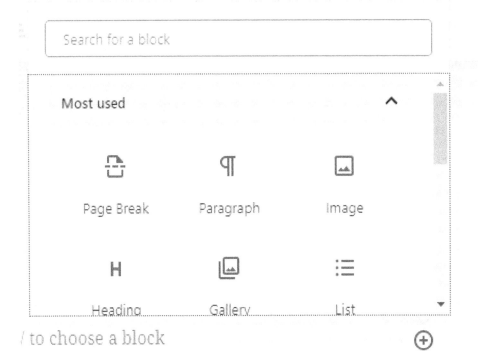

Block Editing Tools

There are some tools that you can use to edit your **Page** in the **Block Editor.** At the top of the screen is the Block Editor Toolbar, which features many icons that you can use to edit your page. These Toolbars include;

- **The Add Block tab** ⊕ : You will be able to deploy this icon to add a new block in your text. When you click on this icon, you will receive a popup that will enable access to various types of block that you can use on your website or blog.

- **The Undo tab** ↺ : Tap on this icon to undo any change you have made recently.

- **The Redo tab** ↻ : Redo what you have undone.

- **The Content Structure** ⓘ : This will bring information about the content of your page. It will normally show you the number of headings, paragraphs, words, and blocks that are in your content.

- **The Block Navigation tab** ≡ : All the blocks present in your content will be shown here and a link will be available for each of the blocks.

- **The Tools tab** ✎ : The **Tools** tab gives various interactions for block selection and editing. Use the **Select** tool to help you to choose Blocks. Once you have chosen a block, tap the Enter key to bring the **Edit** tool.

- **The Switch to draft tab** Switch to draft : The **Switch to Draft** button will show right after you have published your Page/Post. Click on this menu to unpublish your post/page and reverse to draft mode.

- **The Save Draft icon** Save Draft : This icon will allow you to save your Page and will only appear if you are yet to publish your page or post.

- **The Preview button** Preview : You can preview your page by clicking on this icon. This will open a new browser window.

- **The Publish button** Publish... : This button enables you to publish your post/page when you are done writing your posts or editing your pages. The latest version of WordPress (WP version 5.5.1) used in this guide makes use of two steps methods for publishing your contents. After you have finished writing your contents and tapping on the publish icon, you will be redirected to a new panel with a confirmation prompt and a new publish button. The new panel will let you modify the content visibility and choose the time and data you want your content to go live. You can make the post public or set the post to be readable only by the admin. When you click on the second publish button, you will be able to publish your post/page and get your content across to the public.

- **The update icon** Update : Immediately your post/page has been published, the publish icon discussed above will quickly change to an **Update icon.** You will be able to save changes you made to contents by clicking on the **Update icon.**

- **The Settings Sidebar** ⚙ : Brings all important settings for your Post or Page including elements such as adding featured Images, specifying your Categories and Tags on Posts, or selecting Page/Post templates. You can tap on the **Settings** tab if you want to show and hide the settings sidebar.

- **The More tools & options icon** ⋮ : This is mostly the last icon in the Toolbar. **The More tools & options icon** gives access to more ad hoc settings. You will be able to activate or deactivate the **Top Toolbar** and **Spotlight Mode**. In addition, you will be able to show your web contents with the **Visual Editor (**which is mostly the default way of adding blocks) or with the **Code Editor (**to edit the underlying html). You can equally display your web content using the **Visual Editor** (which is the default mode for adding blocks) or using the **Code Editor**, which enables you to improve and edit the underlying html. You will be able to navigate the list of editor keyboard shortcuts and copy your entire page's content with a single click.

Right below the **Block Editor Toolbar** is your **Content area** which will allow you to write your contents (much like you would with a Microsoft Word).

Your contents will be made up of different block type; and for every block you add inside the content space, there exists a toolbar which is normally display by default above the block or inside the main Block Editor Toolbar at the top of your screen (you need to turn on the Top Toolbar option from the **more option icon).** You can also enjoy the distraction free mode by tapping the full screen mode highlighted in the image below from the **more option icon.** The full screen mode will remove all the features displayed above the content area so that you won't necessarily be distracted with them. See image below;

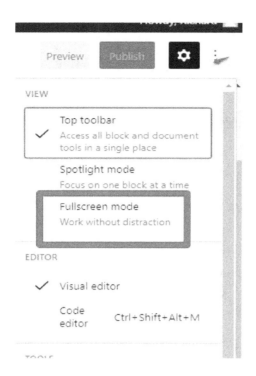

Next to your **content space** on the right navigation pane is the **settings** side bar. The **settings** side bar will allow you to do some settings for the entire post or page, which you are currently working on. The **settings** side bar also features settings that are specific for the currently selected block.

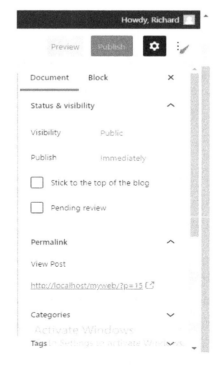

When you look at the bottom of the **settings** sidebar, you will see two tabs that you can select from which include the **Document** tab and the **Block** tab. The **Document** tab will allow you access to the settings for the entire post or page you are currently working on.

The **Document** tab features the following settings;

- **Status & visibility**: Here, you will be able to modify your post's visibility and indicate the specific time and date you want the post to be published. To choose a publishing time for your post, expand the **Status & visibility** dropdown and tap on the "**immediately** – default publishing time" link beside publish. By tapping on the **"Immediately"** link, you will be prompted with a screen where you can select the exact date and time you want the post to go live.

In the same vein, you will be able to adjust your content's visibility by choosing between **public (visible to everyone), Private (only visible to site admin and editors)** and **Password protected (protected with a password you choose. Only those with the password can view this post).** The default visibility setting is always **Public.**

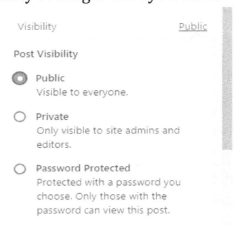

- **Permalink:** This is the complete address that houses your post, page and any other content on your blog or website. The permalink can contain your website domain name together with a slug. A slug just any other part of the web address that usually follows the domain name. You can use the date you wrote the post as the slug – remember slug is just anything that follows the domain name – or just anything at all (probably the title of the post). In the image below, the title of the content (about god) has been used as slug and you can tap on the link below the **"View page"** to see the post once you have published it.

- **Featured image:** This part will allow you to set featured images for your post. To do this, simply click on the "**set featured image**" box and you will be taken to a page where you can choose any file you want to use as your featured image. Select between **upload files (**this allows you to upload an image from your computer as featured image) and **Media library (**contains preloaded images for you).

- **Discussion section:** This section will allow or disable comments on your posts. You can enable comments on your post by tapping on the "**allow comment**" box right below the **Discussion** tab. To disable comment, simply uncheck the box.

- **Categories section:** Add categories to your post. If you do not add a post category, your post will appear on the live blog as uncategorized.

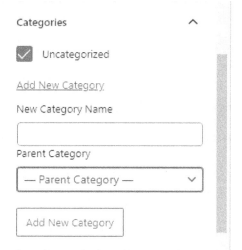

- **Tags:** Add keywords that you used for topics. Tags are very specific and unique to the contents in your post. For instance, let us assume that you write something on Leo Patrick, the popular blogger in California; you can set up the tag as Leo Patrick, blogger. You can add as many tags to your post as it can contain; just make sure they are specific to your post and rather not broad.

The **Block tab** brings settings for the active block (block that you are currently working on). When you click on the **Add Block +** icon located at the left navigation pane of the **Add new page** section, you will be prompted with the list of available blocks and you will see the **Block** tab at the right hand side changing almost immediately; this depends on the type of block you are working with under the "**add block**" section. Tap on the "**+**" sign at the top to navigate and see the list of available blocks.

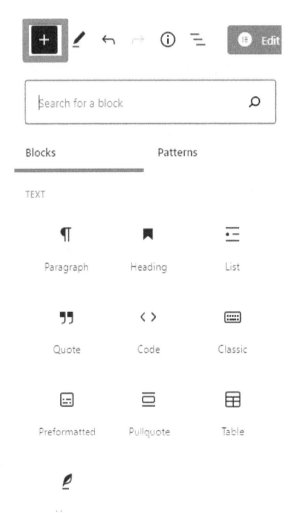

The following types of blocks are common;

- **Page Break:** This divides your content to look like a multi-page experience.
- **Paragraph:** This features settings that you can use to change text size, text's background color and whether to display Drop cap. When you activate the Drop cap button, you can permit texts to display a large initial letter.

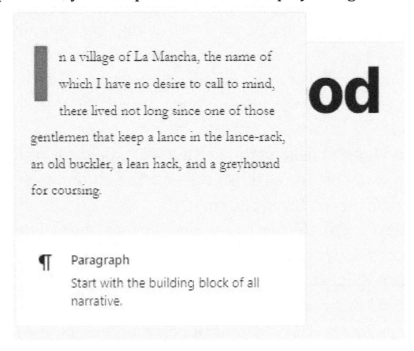

- **Gallery:** This displays multiple images in a rich gallery.
- **Image:** Here, you will be able to insert your images for best text's representation.
- **Headings:** Here, you will be able to introduce new content and arrange your contents to allow visitors and search engines to comprehend how your contents are structured.
- **List:** Use this to make a bullet or number list.
- **Quote:** Give emphasis to quoted statements in your text.
- **Audio:** This is used to embed a simple audio player.
- **Cover:** This can be used to insert an image or video with a text overlay.

The Block Editor options

You can access different options that are available to allow you to set how you want your Block Editor to be coming up. You will be able to see these options by navigating to the "**More tools & options**" icon at the right side of the page whenever you are editing your post or page. You will get the following menu by tapping on the "**More tools & options**" icon;

- **Top Toolbar** – Tapping on this will allow you to see all blocks and documents tools in a single place. Un-checking this option will display some tools at the top and some few other tools right below the title of your Post.
- **Spotlight Mode** – This mode will allow you to focus one block at a time by deactivating all the blocks on the page except the current block you are working on.
- **Fullscreen Mode** - Enabling this setting will hide the top admin bar and the left-hand menu. This is much like the Distraction-free writing mode, which was present in the old Classic Editor.
- **Visual Editor** - This setting is usually activated by default and will bring your content as individual blocks.
- **Code Editor** - Enable this option to turn off the Visual Editor and instead bring the html that make up your content. It is necessary to understand that whilst you still have HTML in your underlying content, the new Block editor equally wraps each individual section of your post/page within HTML comment tags. It utilizes these comment tags to constitute a difference between the different types of blocks that makes up your content within. Although, you will be able to edit the HTML that is displaying your content by deploying the **Code Editor,** which is found within the Block Editor, you must still be careful so that you don't remove or edit any part of the HTML that built your contents. Removing or editing any part of the HTML comments that constituted your content will lead to one or more of your blocks not showing properly as soon as you switch back to the Visual Editor mode. This may make you lose your web contents.
- **Block Manager** - This setting will allow you to deactivate individual blocks or the entire block panels. This restricts them from being displayed within the Block Inserter. You, as the admin of the post and the website won't have access to see a block once you have disabled it. Nevertheless, every other user on the blog will still be able to access the deactivated block.

- **Manage All Reusable Blocks** – Clicking on this will automatically exit you from the Block Editor interface and you will then be prompted with a list of all blocks that are reusable which you can edit, export them to a file (you can import them later to another site) or delete them. Endeavor to save your contents before tapping on this option, as you won't be prompted to save any page before you are taken directly to the list of reusable blocks. You can lose all of your contents if you don't save them before exit.
- **Keyboard Shortcuts** – Provides you with the list of all the available keyboard shortcuts that are deployable within the Block Editor.
- **Welcome Guide** - Gives you concise information concerning the Block Editor and what it is used for.
- **Copy All Content** – You will be able to copy all your contents within the active page or post straight to the clipboard.
- **Help** – The welcome guide is not very detailed most times and the Help menu will normally give a link to some external website pages where you can access more comprehensive information of how to deploy the Block Editor and what the Block Editor actually does.
- **Options** - This menu provides more options that you can utilize to customize how the Block Editor displays. You can disable or enable the Pre-publish Checks, the Inserter Help Panel and a wide variety of other Panels, coupled with many default Document Panels such as the Tags, Categories or Featured Image Panels.

CHAPTER TWO

ADDING CONTENTS WITH BLOCK

The new Block Editor consists of page's contents with blocks of different type. Each of the content on your page will actually consist of different block while each paragraph will consist of separate block. The Block Editor features blocks for all of your common contents like headings, paragraphs, ordered and unordered Lists (i.e. bullet points), images, quotes, galleries and any other content that can be done with the old TinyMCE Classic Editor. Inserting blocks inside your contents can be done in a number of ways. The most common method of adding blocks in your content is clicking on the "**Add block icon⊕**" in the Block Toolbar located at the top section of the screen. Tapping on the ⊕ will bring the Block Inserter popup, which is the panel that gets you access to all the various categories of blocks that you can use in your contents. You can quickly scroll through the list of the block displayed and choose the block that you will like to insert, or alternatively use the search bar at the top of the screen to search for the block and filter the list. While using the Block inserter at the top of the screen, you will see an **Inserter Help Panel** on the right hand side of the inserter. When you move the cursor over each block on the list, you will get a small preview of that particular block in the **inserter help panel** on the right navigation pane.

If you cannot see the help panel at the right hand side, or if you can otherwise see the panel but you would like to hide it from view, you can deactivate or activate by deploying the **options** panel. To see the **options** panel, tap on the **Options** menu available under the "**More tools & options**" icon located at the top right side of the screen. Once you see the **Options** panel, tap the **Inserter help panel** box to activate or deactivate it. The different categories of blocks available in the popup panel are grouped into different sections based on their type, and you can either show or conceal each section by clicking on the arrow icon beside each section title. Once you choose a block to insert it and there are no other available blocks on the page that are selected, then the new block you chose will be appended right to the bottom of your content, just below all the existing blocks in the page. If you have a block selected in your page when you insert a new block, the new block will be inserted below your previously selected block.

Another method of inserting block in your content is by clicking on the **Add block** ⊕shown at the top area of the individual block. You will be able to see the **add block**⊕ by moving your cursor across the top border of each block. Tapping on the ⊕ will bring the Block Inserter popup, which is the panel that gets you access to all the various categories of blocks that you can use in your contents. You can quickly scroll through the list of the block displayed and choose the block that you will like to insert, or alternatively use the search bar at the top of the screen to search for the block and filter the list. The different categories of blocks available in the popup panel are grouped into different sections based on their type, and you can either show or conceal each section by clicking on the arrow icon beside each section title. Once you choose a block to insert it and there are no other available blocks on the page that are selected, then the new block you chose will be appended right to the bottom of your content, just below all the existing blocks in the page. If you have a block selected in your page when you insert a new block, the new block will be inserted above the previous block.

You can as well add an entirely new block by utilizing the **Add block** icon below the content you are developing. Supposing the last Block in your content is not a paragraph block, there will be an empty Paragraph Block located at the bottom of your content. It is good to understand that if this last block is actually a Paragraph Block, then you will not see the empty Paragraph Block at the bottom of your content by default as you will need to either hit the enter key in your last block to bring the empty paragraph block, or utilize any of the previously discussed methods to add a new block. If there exists an empty paragraph block below your content and you wish to add a new text paragraph, then you need to place the cursor inside the empty block and start writing your content. If you wish to change from this new block to an entirely different block, you can tap on the **Add block** icon you see on the side of the empty Paragraph Block. Tapping on the ⊕ will bring the Block Inserter popup, which is the panel that gets you access to all the various categories of blocks that you can use in your contents. You can quickly scroll through the list of the block displayed and choose the block that you will like to insert, or alternatively use the search bar at the top of the screen to search for the block and filter the list. The different categories of blocks available in the popup panel are grouped into different sections based on their type, and you can either show or conceal each section by clicking on the arrow icon beside each section title. Once you choose a block to add it, the empty paragraph block will be changed to the new block that you want.

Every block possesses its own toolbar menu that is shown at the top part of the block (or found at the top part of the screen if you have already activated the **Top Toolbar** option). The **More options** icon on this toolbar has two options for adding blocks, "**Insert Before" and "Insert After**." Selecting any of these options will add an empty Paragraph Block either above or below the current block respectively. As discussed previously, you can start typing inside this empty block if you wish to add a new text paragraph, or you can switch this empty Paragraph Block to a new block type entirely by tapping on the **Add block** icon located on the side of the block.

More about the Block Editor

Using the **Block Editor,** each block you are working on will have a "**More options** ⋮ " icon shown at the top of each selected block. The "**More options** ⋮ " icon will allow you to;

- Reveal or conceal the block settings: You can hide the block settings (the block setting for each selected block is always shown at the right navigation pane) by tapping on the "**More options**" icon at the top of the specific block you have selected and then choose the "**Hide Block settings.**" Bring back the block settings by tapping once again on the "**Hide Block settings.**"

- Duplicate the block you are currently working on: To double the current block, tap on **"Duplicate."** Duplicated blocks will normally look like the image below;

- If you wish to add a new block just before the active block (the block you are currently working on), choose the ***Insert before*** menu
- If you wish to add a new block just after the active block (the block you are currently working on), choose the ***Insert after*** menu.
- If you wish to add the active block to the list of reusable blocks, tap on the **"Add to Reusable blocks"** menu.
- Tap on the **"Group"** menu to add block to groups.
- Tap on the **"Remove block"** option to remove active block.

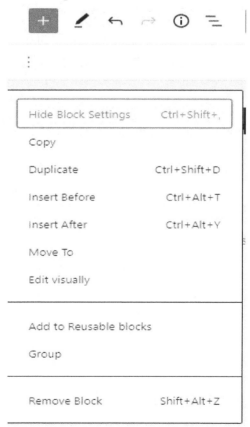

The Block inserter icon

By tapping on the **Block inserter icon "+,"** you can move through some lists of sections. These sections contain blocks and features, which drive home the essence of the Block Editor interface. The sections include;

- **TEXTS:** Contains some basic blocks such as paragraph, heading, list, quote, classic, preformatted, Pull quote, verse and Table block.

- **MEDIA BLOCKS:** Contains useful blocks such as image, gallery, audio, cover, file, video and media & texts. These blocks are used to add media files into your contents.
- **DESIGN:** This features more blocks that are made for special purposes. It includes blocks such as Buttons, column, group, more, page break, separator and spacer.
- **WIDGETS:** Contains Shortcode, archive, calendar, categories, custom HTML, latest comments, latest posts, RSS, search, social icon and Tag cloud.
- **EMBEDS:** Contains menus such as Twitter, Facebook, Instagram, YouTube etc. This block allows you to add contents from social media inside your blog contents.

These blocks highlighted above perform functions ranging from adding video files, audio files, images, social media contents etc inside your content. Let us take a look at what some of the important blocks can help users to achieve;

- **Audio block:** The audio block will allow users to add an audio file inside their content. To add an audio file, select **audio** under the "**TEXT**" block. Once you tap on the audio block, click on the **upload** tab to add an audio file from your computer inside your content. If you choose the **media library** option, you will be able to have access to your media library and choose from audio files that you have used before. Selecting the **Insert from URL tab** will allow you to upload audio files from an existing URL. Once you have added the audio file successfully, you can select **auto play** from the settings bar so that the audio file can be played automatically once anybody visits your website or select **loop** to continuously loop the audio over and over.

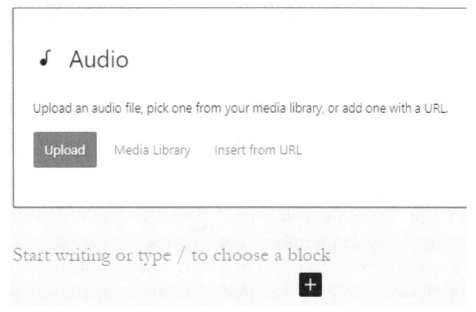

- **Cover Block:** This will enable you to add a video or an image inside your content and allow you to optionally add color overlay and text. Once you have added the video or image successfully, you can then add a text over the image by tapping on the **write title...** inside the added video or image. Also, navigate to the **settings** sidebar at the right hand side to have access to an array of customized settings. Tap on the **fixed background** option to set the video or image as a background video or image. Whenever readers/visitors scroll over your contents, the page will start sliding over the top of the image or video in the background. If you don't select the **fixed background** option here, the background text or video will start moving along with the other part of your contents on your page. You can also pick an overlay color by choosing between the **solid color and the gradient** color option. The **background opacity** slider can be used to increase or reduce the opacity of the selected color. This will help you tint the added image or video making the text look unique.
- **File Block:** Once you select the **File block** under the **Media block,** you can insert a new file (PDF or Word document) inside your post by clicking on the **upload** link. You can also choose the **media library** option to bring your

media library and then choose from any of the files that you have previously used. Once you have added your file successfully, you can select any setting from the right navigation pane of the screen. For instance, if you want to link the media file or to the WordPress attachment page, simply tap on the "**link to**" dropdown from settings and choose either media file or attachment page. If you want the file to open in a new window once your site visitor taps on it to download, simply toggle on the "**open in new tab**" option. In the same vein, toggle on the "**show download button**" to display the download button for the file on your website.

- **Gallery Block:** With the gallery block, you can add an image gallery into your content. To use the gallery block, select the "**gallery block**" under the **media block.** Tap on the **upload** button if you want to upload images from your computer to the media library. You can choose from an already uploaded image by selecting the **media library** option. In fact, you can drag and drop images from your computer into the gallery block. Once the image has been uploaded successfully, switch to the settings bar at the right navigation pane to gain access to various settings that can be customized for the uploaded image. Tap on the **crop** ⌐ icon at the top if you want to crop and align the image properly. Tap on the **image size** dropdown on the settings side to choose the image size (you can select from thumbnail, medium and full size). You can place your cursor on the **write caption...** under each uploaded image to write a caption for each image. Specify the dimension for the image by entering the height and width value inside the **image dimension** section. Choose the default style of the image under the **default style (**you can choose either default style or rounded).

- **Heading Block:** This block can be used to introduce new sections and properly organize your content so that visitors and search engines can easily understand the structure of your content. The heading block has some settings - at the right hand side - such as Typography settings, color settings, text settings and advanced settings. You will be able to adjust color for texts by choosing the **color settings** tab. The **text color** under the color setting will change the color for the text (you can see the text heading changing color at the left hand side as you select colors) while the **background color** changes the background for the text heading. Tapping on the **custom color** link to customize your desired color. Tap on the "**Advanced section**" to insert an HTML anchor, which provides a unique web address for your heading and gives the link to access that particular part of your page.

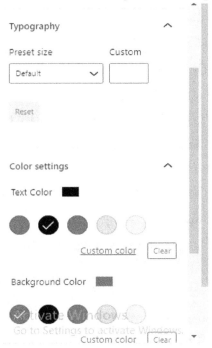

- **Image block:** Allows you to insert an image to make a visual statement. Once you tap on the Image block, click on the **upload** tab to add an image file from your computer inside your content. If you choose the **media library** option, you will be able to have access to your media library and choose from image files that you have used before. Selecting the **Insert from URL tab** will allow you to upload an image file from an existing URL. You can equally utilize the drag and drop button to drag and drop any image into the image block, which will be automatically uploaded into the media library and added into the block. Once the image has been uploaded successfully, switch to the settings bar at the right navigation pane to gain access to various settings that can be customized for the uploaded image.

Tap on the **crop** ⬑ icon at the top if you want to crop and align the image properly. Tap on the **image size** dropdown on the settings side to choose the image size (you can select from thumbnail, medium and full size). You can place your cursor on the **write caption...** under each uploaded image to write a caption for each image. Specify the dimension for the image by entering the height and width value inside the **image dimension** section. Choose the default style of the image under the **default style (**you can choose either default style or rounded).

- **List Block:** The **List Block** allows users to add ordered and unordered lists (i.e. bullet points) inside their content. Once you have successfully added the list items, you can use the appropriate icon on the Block Toolbar to move between an ordered list and an unordered list. If you have chosen an Ordered List (sometimes also called a numbered list), there are varieties of options available in the Settings Sidebar.

- **Paragraph Block:** The **Paragraph Block** allows users to enter a paragraph for their content. Each paragraph stands for a new block, which translates, that when you hit the Enter key to initiate a new paragraph; a new Paragraph Block will be automatically inserted as you continue to write your content. Once you have added the content to your *Paragraph Block*, there are many other options available in the Settings bar. You will be able to change text's size by using the **Preset size** dropdown (you will be able to choose between defaults, small, normal, large, huge and even customize your text's size) or set a custom size yourself by using the **Custom** number field next to the **Preset size** dropdown. The **Drop Cap** switch allows users to change the first character in the paragraph to a Drop Cap (show a very large initial capital letter). The Drop Caps are frequently deployed to get readers' attention. You will only see the Drop cap if you have chosen the block. When you are writing content inside the paragraph block, or you are merely trying to edit existing content, the first character will show the same size just like the rest of the paragraph text. You can change the background color and the text color with the **color settings** in the settings sidebar. By default, there are wide varieties of pre-selected colors you can select from as well as a custom color selector, for choosing any color you want. Depending on the current theme, the available colors may be slightly different from the default color, so that the style within that specific theme can be matched. If the color match that you select for the background and text color is difficult to read, you will see a warning telling you that **"This color combination may be hard for people to read. Try using a brighter background color and/or a darker text color".** You can proceed to change the color to a more suitable one.

CHAPTER THREE

SAVING AND PUBLISHING YOUR CONTENT

Saving and publishing is perhaps the next thing for most people after writing good content on a blog. However, it is worth remembering that you can initially save your post as **draft** (if you are still planning to revise the post at a later time) or **publish** the post immediately if you are convinced that the post is okay for readers'. If you want to save your post as draft, simply click on the **safe draft** link at the top of the screen. If the post is one that you have previously published, you won't be able to see the **safe draft** link at the top of the screen. Instead, you would see a **switch draft** link. Un-publish the post by tapping on the **switch draft** link; this will revert the post to draft mode and you can now see the **safe draft** link at the top of the page. If you wish to have a feel of how your post will appear on your website when you finally publish it, click on the **preview** link. If you want to allow another editor/writer to edit your content on your behalf before you finally make the post public, tap on the **pending review** under the **status & visibility** menu in the **settings** sidebar. This will make your post editable by another editor you give access to. To make this particular post/content you are working on stick to the top of the other posts on your website, click on the "**stick to the top of the blog**" checkbox under the **status & visibility** menu in the **settings** sidebar. This can only be done for posts and not for pages.

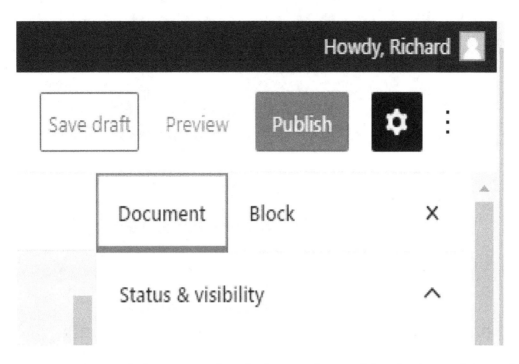

To edit your post's visibility, simply click on the **public** link to the right of the **visibility** setting under the **status & visibility** panel. You can choose from any of the following post's/page's visibility setting;

• **Public:** This represents the default setting and tapping on this will let your post/page be visible to everyone that visits your blog.

• **Private:** Tapping on the **private** link will hide your content and nobody else will see the page/post on your blog. Readers and visitors on your blog won't be notified of hidden contents. You are the only person that can see hidden posts on your blog.

• **Password Protected:** Allows you to prompt a password to your page. Only readers or people with the password will have access to the content on your page.

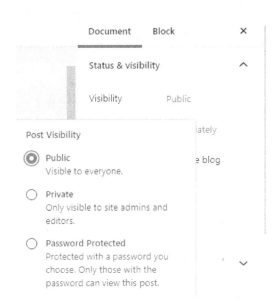

Under the **Permalink** panel in the **Settings Sidebar**, the full URL for your post will be displayed. This URL will be accessible once you have saved your post for the first time, and it will be accompanied by the post's slug (visit the previous sections to see how we discussed the slug) that was generated automatically for the post. Tapping on this URL will take you to the published page of your post or the preview page if you have not published the post yet. You will be able to edit the slug page by clicking on the URL slug field above the URL link. When you edit the slug link appropriately, you have the chance to improve the SEO (search engine optimization) for your post or page. This means that when people search for contents that you have on search engines, your website will be among the websites that pops up first. You can as well decide to make use of the default page URL generated by WordPress for your post, only that this might not boost the SEO for the post. WordPress makes use of your post's title to generate a post's link for you. This means you can even make your post's title SEO compliant by using keywords that readers are mostly interested in.

By default, whenever you publish your Page/Post, your post is usually published immediately as this is the default setting. You can change this setting by tapping on the **"always show pre-publish check"** link located just below the "pre-publish" alert page (a page you will be taken to once you tap on publish at the top of the page) under the **Visibility** panel.

You can then select the time and date that you desire your content to be published. After you set the time and date to publish your post, you will still have to click on the **publish** button located at the top of the screen so that your content will be published on the chosen date and time. When you click on the **publish** button at the top, you will be prompted with a publish notification alert allowing you to confirm whether you plan to publish the post or not on the chosen date and time.

The publish notification page will as well let you edit the post's visibility (public, private and password protected), schedule publishing time and date and to add tags (which will let your website's visitors and relevant search engines navigate your content quickly just with the right keywords you added). You can disallow the publish notification page from always coming up by un-checking the "**Always show pre-publish check**" at the bottom of the publish notification section. Click on the **publish** link located at the top of the screen to finally publish your post.

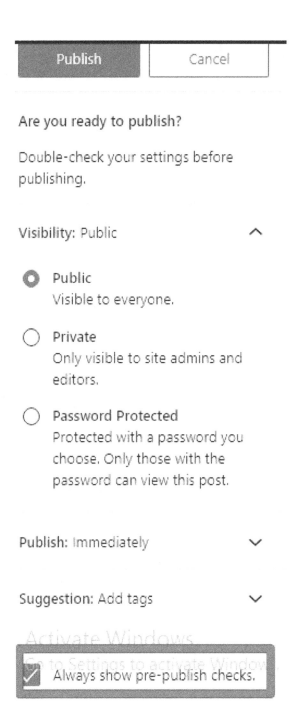

How to edit existing contents

You will be able to edit or improve existing contents of your posts by selecting the specific post's title when you are viewing the list of posts you have published or the ones that are saved as draft. To do this, follow the steps below;

- Scroll to the left navigation pane of the WordPress dashboard and click on **Post.**
- You will be taken to a section that contains the list of posts that you have worked on (posts are arranged with their authors, published date and tags).
- Hover your cursor over the post you want to modify and tap on the **edit** link beneath the title of the post.
- You will be redirected to the section where you can improve or edit your post. Click on the **Update** icon once you finish editing the post.

					2020/09/18 at 7:23 pm
☐ about God Edit Quick Edit Trash View	Richard	Uncategorized	—	—	Published 2020/09/17 at 2:32 pm
☐ Hello world!	Richard	Uncategorized	—	1	Published 2020/08/02 at 10:26 pm

How to delete posts or pages

To delete your post or page, kindly follow the steps below;

- Scroll to the left navigation pane of the WordPress dashboard and click on **Post.**
- You will be taken to a section that contains the list of posts that you have worked on (posts are arranged with their authors, published date and tags).
- Hover your cursor over the post that you want to delete and tap on the **trash** link beneath the title of the post.
- Taping the trash link will take your post or page to the trash.

You can actually delete the post or page permanently or choose to restore the post or page you have sent to the trash by choosing the **trash** icon located at the top section of your post. Hover your cursor on the post or page that you plan to delete permanently and the **restore and delete permanently link** will pop up beneath the title of the post. Click on the **delete permanently** to permanently delete a page or post. Click on **restore** to get back the post you have deleted. If you prefer to permanently delete or restore many posts all at once, choose the checkboxes beside each post you wish to delete or restore and then tap on either **Restore** or **Delete Permanently** from the **Bulk Actions** dropdown list at the top of the page. When you have chosen the appropriate action, click on the **Apply** button to carry out what you want. You can alternatively choose the **Empty Trash** button if you want to delete all posts or pages in the Trash.

Comments

The comment section is one of the features at the left hand side of the WordPress dashboard. Your audiences will be able to express their views about your post with the help of the comment box added to your post. Comment brings some kind of author-reader relationship where the author of a post is able to understand what the readers want and how they feel about the whole page. However, as the owner, you get control over what readers post on the comment box and you can even disable the comment box totally preventing readers from expressing their views. You can make comments queued for your approval before they are visible on the website. This way you can control and disregard harmful comments and comments you consider irrelevant to the post. To see the list of all the comments that have been made on your posts throughout, simply click on **Comments** menu. At the top of the comment screen are links that you can leverage to filter comments to only show comments that are approved, pending, marked as spam or in the trash. A number will be quoted in brackets indicating how many there are for each category of pending comments, approved comments, spam comments and trashed comments.

When you hover your cursor over each comment that has been made in the comment list, the following links will be available beneath the comment;

Comment

Hi, this is a comment.
To get started with moderating, editing, and deleting comments, please visit the Comments screen in the dashboard. Commenter avatars come from Gravatar.

Unapprove   Reply   Quick Edit   Edit   Spam   Trash

Comment

- **Unapprove/Approve** – Select this option if you want to unapprove a comment that has been previously approved for a particular post. The comment you have unapproved will no longer be available on your website. If your cursor is on a comment that you have previously unapproved, then you will see **approve** instead of **unapprove** giving you another chance to approve such comment.
- **Reply** – If you want to write a reply to specifically address that comment, simply click on the **reply** option.
- **Quick Edit** – To **quickly** edit the email, name, URL and the actual comment of the commenter, simply tap on this option.
- **Edit** – Choosing this option will allow you to edit the email, name, URL and the comment made by the commenter. It also enables you to mark the comment as either approved, Spam or pending and to also modify the date and time that the comment was made.
- **Spam** – Mark any comment as spam by tapping on the **spam** option.
- **Trash** – Take a comment to the trash by tapping on this option. Any comment that has been trashed can be restored or deleted permanently from the trash.

Replying to a comment

Sometimes, you might wish to reply to a particular comment made on your post; whether to clarify something or to appreciate the person who sent the comment. To do this, hover your cursor over the comment and a **reply** link will pop up. You will then see an edit field below the comment where you can enter your reply.

Editing a Comment

Editing any particular comment can be done by hovering your mouse over the comment and selecting the **Quick Edit** link or tapping on the **Edit** link. Actually, both options perform the same thing; the only difference is that the **Edit** link will also allow you to mark the comment as pending, approved or spam and to modify the date and time the comment was made.

Unapproving and Approving Comment Made On Your Post

There are tons of visitors coming to read contents on your website every day, and going by this you may likely see some harsh comments or racist comments from unhappy readers' who just want to lash out for no reason. If that is the case, then you can decide to un-approved such a comment. To unapprove a comment, kindly position your cursor over the comment until you see the **Unapprove** link popping up. Click on **Unapprove** to unapprove the comment. Unapproved comments will be displayed with a different background color on the list of comments. Unapproved comments will also have a red vertical stripe down the left side of the row. Hovering the cursor over the comment will bring an **Approve** link instead of an **Unapprove** link.

Marking a Comment as Trash or Spam

If you see that a spam comment has been passed on your post, you can choose to mark the comment as spam, by hovering the cursor of your computer over the comment and tapping on the **Spam** link. If you are utilizing the Akismet plugin and you noticed a spam comment that Akismet missed, you can mark the comment as spam by yourself to enable Akismet learn so that it won't miss to mark such types of comments as spam in the future. To delete a particular comment, simply hover your cursor over the comment and choose **Trash.**

You can empty the Trash by clicking on the **Trash** link at the top part of the page to bring all the comments that have been marked as Trash. This link will be displayed together with a number within brackets to indicate how many comments have been marked as Trash. To permanently remove all the comments, click on the **Empty Trash** button. You won't be prompted to confirm your choice to delete.

You can empty the Spam by clicking on the **Spam** link at the top part of the page to bring all the comments that have been marked as **Spam**. This link will be displayed together with a number within brackets to indicate how many comments have been marked as Spam. To permanently remove all the comments, click on the **Empty Spam** button. You won't be prompted to confirm your choice to delete Spam. You can also delete a single spam permanently by choosing the **Delete Permanently** link that pops up when you move your cursor over each row. You won't be prompted to confirm your choice to delete.

Appearance

You can modify and customize the way your website looks and feel by making use of the various menus under this section.

Selecting Your Themes

When you click on the **Appearance** tab, the default themes screen will be prompted. The themes which you are currently using (active themes) will be displayed at the top left hand side of the screen. The other themes shown apart from the active themes are the installed themes but not active at the moment. To view an overview of your page/website in other themes that are not the active themes, kindly choose the **live preview** button embedded on each theme. While your preview screen is still displaying, you will be allowed to tap on your website links in order to access your various pages in the new theme layout and also perform necessary theme changes. To use another theme for your website (other than the active themes), hover your cursor across any themes that you want to use and click on the **Activate** link that pops up beneath each theme. Alternatively, if you can still see the preview window, you can tap on the **Save & Activate** button at the top left corner of the preview window to activate the theme. Place your cursor over a theme thumbnail image and select **Theme Details** to access more details about a particular theme. You will be greeted with a window showing a larger view of the themes including the themes description and other important details. When you click on the **Add New** button found at the top section of the screen, or you click on the **Add New Theme** box that shows after all your theme thumbnail images, you will be able to upload a new theme to your website and also install new themes by searching the WordPress Themes Directory.

Adding New Themes

You can add new themes to your page/website straight from the WordPress dashboard. To do this, navigate to the WordPress dashboard, tap on **appearance** and select **Themes.** You will see the "**add new**" button at the top area of the Themes screen where you will be able to search and install new themes on your website. You can manually upload your themes to your website right from the "**add new themes**" page. To upload your chosen theme, choose the **Upload Theme** button at the top part of the page. Select your preferred theme file from your computer by tapping on the **Browse...** button. The Themes file must be added in **.Zip** format. Once you click on the **Install now** button, your themes will be added automatically and then installed on your website. You can preview the theme you just added, activate it or go back to the Themes page.

Users

Under the Users section, you will be able to see and search all existing users on your website. You, as the site administrator, will have access to as many settings and features as possible here, while other site users have restricted functions.

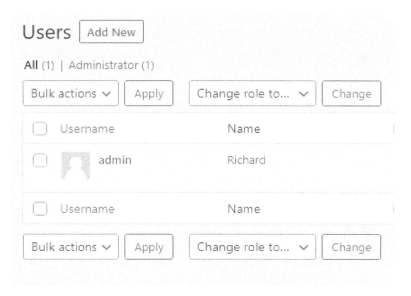

When you move your cursor over each user in the list of users', you will see the following menus beneath the identity of the user;

- **Edit:** Tap on the edit link to edit some information about the user. Details such as **contact info, email, names (not username) and roles** can always be edited for users.
- **Delete:** To delete details for a particular user, simply tap on the **delete** link. You won't be able to delete your own profile as the site admin.

The following are the types of roles, which the site admin can assign to users;

- **Administrator:** This user will have unchallenged access to all of the website's settings and features.
- **Editor:** The editor will be able to publish and manage posts on the website. Posts made by other users can also be managed by an editor.
- **Author:** An author will only be able to publish and manage posts made by him/her.
- **Contributor:** A contributor will be able to write and manage its own post but won't be able to publish the post.
- **Subscriber:** This user will only be able to manage its profile. A subscriber cannot post nor manage a post.

Adding a New User

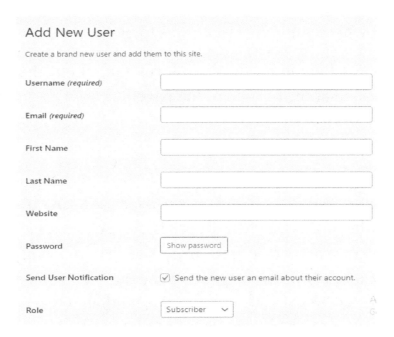

From the WordPress dashboard, tap on the **"add new"** link under the **Users tab** in the left navigation pane. Alternatively, you can click on the "**add new**" tab at the top of the Users page. You will be greeted with a window, which will allow you to fill the basic information below for the user;

- **Username:** It is important that you fill this box. This is the box that contains the username for the new user that you want to add. This username is what the user will be using to log in to the website. Be sure the username is correct before saving the information, as you will not be able to edit it later.
- **Email:** It is also important that you fill this section. Two different users cannot have the same email address. If the user publishes a post, approved comments will be sent to that email address as a notification anytime a reader makes a comment on his post. The email address must be a valid email address.
- You will also be able to input details such as **first name, last name and user's website.**
- **Password:** WordPress will generate a password automatically for this user. Tap on the password box to see the generated password.
- **Send user notification:** Check this box to let WordPress send an email to the user informing them of the account you are creating for them.
- **Role:** This is where you can assign roles to users.

Once you have successfully input all the information about the user, click on the **"add user"** link located at the bottom of the page.

Deleting a User

To delete a particular user from the list, simply click on the **delete** link below the name of the user when you hover the cursor over each row of users. The **delete** link won't be showing if this particular user is currently signed in to the website. When you are deleting a specific user from the list, you will be able to delete contents that have already been assigned to the user. You can select from **delete all contents (**which will delete all contents created by the user) and **attribute all content to (**this will assign all the contents of this particular user to another user you selected using the dropdown list). Click on the **confirm deletion** tab to remove this user.

Categories

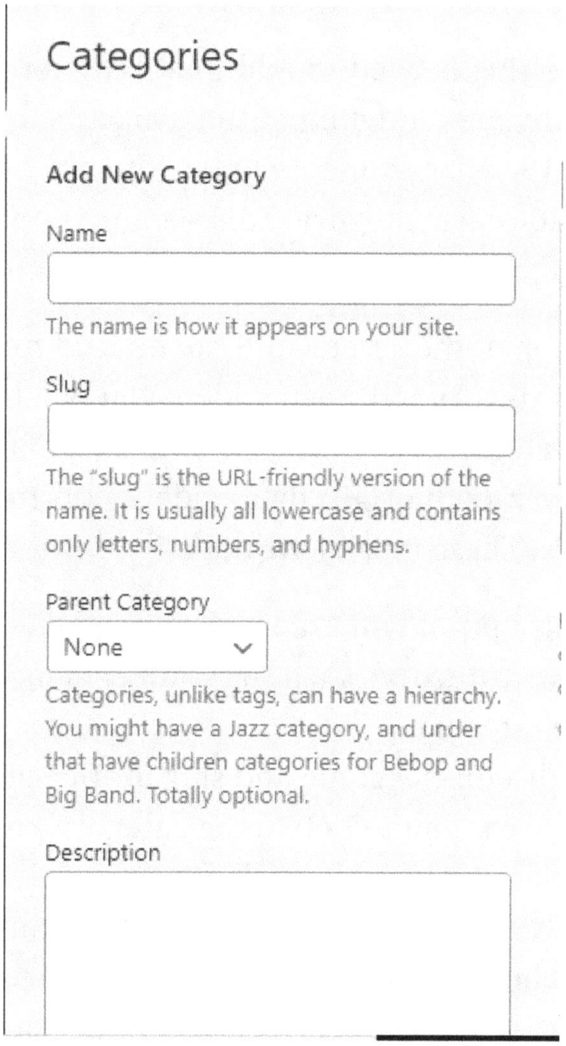

Categories

Add New Category

Name

The name is how it appears on your site.

Slug

The "slug" is the URL-friendly version of the name. It is usually all lowercase and contains only letters, numbers, and hyphens.

Parent Category

None ⌄

Categories, unlike tags, can have a hierarchy. You might have a Jazz category, and under that have children categories for Bebop and Big Band. Totally optional.

Description

To access the **categories** tab, navigate to the WordPress dashboard and tap on the **post** menu. The category tab is used especially to define sections of your blog and group posts that are related. You cannot assign categories to pages but categories can be assigned to posts. You will be able to see the list of the categories you have added when you click on the **category** tab. The following boxes are available under the **category** section;

- **Name:** Input the name of the category just like the way you want it to appear on your website.
- **Slug:** Input the URL –friendly version of the name you added above in this box. You should only enter lower case and must contain only letters, hyphen and numbers.
- **Parent category:** This is used to add hierarchy for your category. You can have students category and under the students category have; students under the age of 10 years, students under the age of 15 years and students under the age of 20 years category. This section is optional.
- **Description:** Add the description for the category inside this box.

Scroll down to the bottom of the screen and tap on **add new category** link to add the category. Once the category has been added, you will be able to see the added category among other categories at the right hand side of the page. Hovering your cursor over each category at the right hand side will bring some menus beneath the name of the category. These menus include;

- **Edit:** Selecting this option will take you to a page where you can edit some properties of the category such as Name, slug, parent category and description of the category.
- **Quick edit:** Quickly edit the name and slug for the added category.
- **Delete:** This will allow you to delete the category permanently from the list of other categories. Once you click on the **delete** menu, you will be prompted to confirm delete. Simply select **OK** if you actually want to delete the category or choose **Cancel** if you don't want to delete the category. Deleting a category will not delete the post under the category.
- **View:** Tapping this will enable you to see the list of posts that are using this category currently.

You can delete more than one categories at a time by tapping on the checkboxes beside the name of the categories you wish to delete and then choose **delete** from the **bulk actions** dropdown located either at the top or the bottom (bulk action is actually available at the top and at the bottom of the page). Upon selecting **delete,** click on the **apply** button to mass delete the selected categories.

Tags

Tags are keywords that you can use to identify genuine information in your posts that may be present or absent in other posts. You cannot assign tags to pages but tags can be assigned to posts. You will be able to see the list of tags you have added when you click on the **tag** tab. The following boxes are available under the **tag** section;

- **Name:** Input the name of the tag just like the way you want it to appear on your website.
- **Slug:** Input the URL –friendly version of the name you added above in this box. You should only enter lower case and must contain only letters, hyphen and numbers.
- **Description:** Add the description for the tag inside this box.

Scroll down to the bottom of the screen and tap on **add new tag** link to add the tag. Once the tag has been added, you will be able to see the added tag among other tags at the right hand side of the page. Hovering your cursor over each tag at the right hand side will bring some menus beneath the name of the tag. These menus include;

- **Edit:** Selecting this option will take you to a page where you can edit some properties of the tag such as Name, slug, and description of the tag.
- **Quick edit:** Quickly edit the name and slug for the added tag.
- **Delete:** This will allow you to delete the tag permanently from the list of other tags. Once you click on the **delete** menu, you will be prompted to confirm delete. Simply select **OK** if you actually want to delete the tag or choose **Cancel** if you don't want to delete the tag. Deleting a tag will not delete the post under the tag.
- **View:** Tapping this will enable you to see the list of posts that are using this tag currently.

You can delete more than one tag at a time by tapping on the checkboxes beside the name of the tags you wish to delete and then choose **delete** from the **bulk**

actions dropdown located either at the top or the bottom (bulk action is actually available at the top and at the bottom of the page). Upon selecting **delete,** click on the **apply** button to mass delete the selected tags.

The Media Panel

This is the panel directly below the **post panel** in the WordPress dashboard. It features the **media library section** and the **Add new section.**

The Media Library

Tapping on the **media library** will allow you access to all the files you have uploaded previously. Choose the **Grid view** ⊞ icon at the top of the screen to view all your media in a grid view, and you can select the **list view** ☰ icon to see all of your media in a list format. You can use the "**All media items**" dropdown at the top of the screen to choose which media item you want to see (whether audio, images, videos, documents etc). In the same vein, use the "**All dates**" dropdown at the top of the screen to select the range of dates for media you want to see. When you hover your cursor over each item on the **list view**, you will be prompted with some links at the bottom of the file's name;

- **Edit:** Tap on this link to edit some media's properties such as title, alt text, description and caption.

- **Delete permanently:** Tap on this link to delete your media permanently from the media gallery.
- **View:** You will be taken to the display page for the media you have chosen.

Add New Tab

There are two ways to add new media in your contents; either by using the "**add new**" located beneath the media section of the WordPress dashboard or using the "**add new**" option located beside the media library (when you tap on the library from the dashboard). If you wish to add a new media to the Media Library, click on the **Add New** link in the left navigation section of the WordPress dashboard or choose the "**Add New**" button at the top of the media library page. If you tap on the **Add New** button at the top of the Media Library page in the **List View mode**, or you choose the **Add New** link in the navigation menu of the WordPress dashboard, you will be able to pick and drag your media from your computer into the **Drop files here** box. Your file(s) will be uploaded automatically. Once your media have been uploaded successfully, they will be listed below the file uploader. If you wish to edit the file properties, choose the **Edit** link next to the file.

Editing an Image in the Grid View

Under the **media library page,** scroll to the top section and change the view to **Grid view.**

Select the image that you want to edit by tapping on the image and you will be taken to a window that look like the one below;

Attachment details

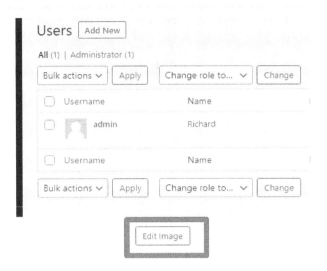

Click on the **edit image** button at the bottom of the image above and you will see the image editing tool window;

- **Crop** | **Crop** – tap on the image and increase or decrease the selection box to suit the exact size that you want the image to be cropped to. Choose the Crop button to crop your image to the new size

- **Rotate left** | Rotate left : Use this icon to rotate the image in the anti-clockwise direction.

- **Rotate right** | Rotate right : Use this icon to rotate the image in the clockwise direction.

- **Flip vertical** [Flip vertical] : Use this icon to flip the image in the vertical orientation.

- **Flip horizontal** [Flip horizontal] : Use this icon to flip the image in the horizontal orientation

- **Undo** [Undo] : undo any previous change

- **Redo** [Redo] : redo any previous change.

Delete an image from the media library in the Grid view

Select the image that you wish to delete to bring the image property section. Then scroll down to the bottom of the page at the right navigation section (image property section) and click on the **delete permanently** link. You will see a prompt to delete messages and you can either cancel the deleting process or delete the image permanently.

Settings

This is used to carry out various settings for your website.

- **General**

Set and configure some basic website preferences such as site title, tag line, WordPress address, administrator email address, and date & time format among other things. You can also choose the default role for new users; this will set the selected role for every new user that you registered. You will also be able to set the site language by tapping on the **site language** box. Tap on **save changes** at the bottom of the screen to save all changes made.

- **Writing**

Here, you can set whether you can post to WordPress via mail, choose default post format and the default post category. To post to WordPress via your mail, you need to set up a secret email account with POP3 access. Any mail received on this mail address will be posted on WordPress, so you need to ensure that the mail is a secret mail.

CHAPTER FOUR

BUILDING WEBSITES WITH ELEMENTOR

In the previous chapters, we have seen how easy it is to create an amazing blog website using the WordPress features. WordPress allows beginners with zero knowledge of programming to create beautiful WordPress websites good enough to anchor their business website (e-commerce), personal websites and websites meant for blog posts. As if that is not intuitive enough, the Elementor page builder provides drag and drop features needed to create visually appealing websites by mere dragging and dropping widgets, features and functions inside your website. Elementor can be installed as a plugin on the WordPress dashboard.

Elementor leverages you to create any type of page ranging from; about pages, landing pages, online stores, full functioning websites etc.

Installing Elementor Page Builder

Before you think of installing the Elementor page builder inside your WordPress to start using many of the amazing WordPress features, you need to be sure whether your computer and version of WordPress can support Elementor as a plugin.

The following are the system required to use Elementor;

- Elementor works best with WordPress version 5.0 and higher. This means you should try to get the latest version of WordPress.
- You will need PHP 7.0 or higher: Although, Elementor works with PHP 5.4+ but web designers have been complaining about security threats and bugs which lower versions of PHP pose to websites. It is always best to upgrade to PHP 7.0 and above.
- You will need MySQL version 5.6 or higher. Elementor can also work with MariaDB version 10.0 or higher.
- You will need a WordPress memory limit of about 128MB. To be on a safer side, use the 256MB.

- Browsers: You will be able to edit your pages with Elementor on browsers like Chrome, Safari, Firefox or Microsoft Edge version 79. You may not be able to edit your pages with an early version of Microsoft Edge. None of the versions of Internet Explorer can edit Elementor pages.
- Devices: You will only be able to edit your pages with Elementor on desktop computers or laptops.

How to Install the Elementor Page Builder

You can add the Elementor page builder into your WordPress by using any of the methods below;

- **From the WordPress dashboard**

You will be able to install Elementor as plugins right from the WordPress dashboard. To do this, follow the prompts below;

- Navigate to the WordPress dashboard, tap on **plugins > Add new.**
- You will be greeted with the plugins page, scroll to the top right hand side and type **Elementor Website builder** in the search bar

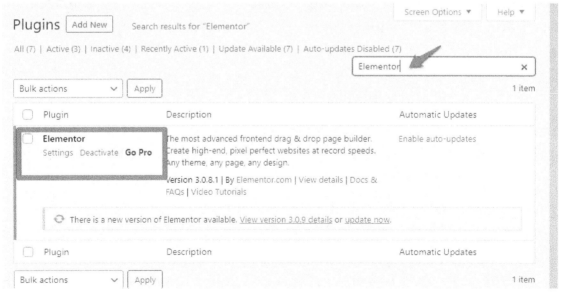

- Although, the Elementor website builder has been installed for me judging from the screenshot above. If you have not previously installed the

Elementor page builder, you will see the **install** menu below the Elementor in the screenshot above.

- Once you have successfully installed the plugins, tap on the **activate** link to integrate Elementor in your WordPress dashboard. You will see the Elementor plugins on your dashboard just like the way it appears in the image below;

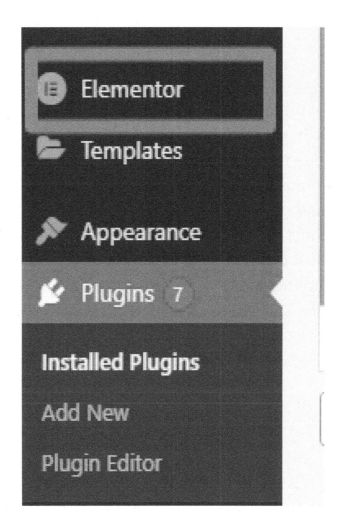

Installing Elementor Via Elementor.Com

- Go to the Elementor website at https://elementor.com/features/editor/. and click on the **get started link.**
- You will be greeted with a window trying to confirm if you already have a WordPress website or not.

Do You Have a WordPress Website?

No, I don't

No problem. We'll help you set up your site

CONTINUE

Yes, I sure do

Great! Click below to install Elementor on your existing website

CONTINUE

ⓘ Why do I need WordPress?

- For users that already have WordPress websites, simply tap on the "**Yes, I sure do**" link. If you don't have a WordPress website, tap on the **"Continue"** link to get you started on creating a WordPress website. We have already discussed various ways of creating a WordPress website in this guide; kindly refer to the previous chapters.

- Once you tap on the "**Yes, I sure do**" link, you will be greeted with a "**Please insert your full domain address.**" This window will verify if you actually have a functioning WordPress website like you claimed. Kindly enter your domain address and click on the "**Check for WordPress**" link.

Please insert your full domain address

For example: http://www.**yourdomain**.com

e.g https://www.elementor.com/

CHECK FOR WORDPRESS

- The **'Install Elementor on your website'** page will be prompted, kindly tap on the **"click to install"** link to log in to your website.
- Once you log in to your website successfully, you will see a page trying to tell you more about Elementor. Click on **install now** to install Elementor in your WordPress website.
- Click on the **activate plugins** link on the displayed page.
- You will get a **thank you** page where you can get started with Elementor.

Free Elementor Vs Elementor Pro

The free Elementor is what you have previously installed on your WordPress dashboard with the **plugins > Add new** method. The free Elementor might be enough for designers planning to create just some simple website page, and buying the Elementor Pro might not be that important for them. On a different note, if you are planning to get more done in WordPress website, then it might be better to buy the Elementor Pro version which gives you more widgets and functions. Sometimes, you can use only the Elementor interface to build your website without deploying any other menu from the WordPress dashboard. There are many Elementor plans to choose from on their website depending on your budget. The lowest Elementor plan goes for 49USD/ year Elementor Pro plan.

How to Install Elementor Pro

- Go to my.elementor.com once you have purchased the Elementor Pro plan.
- Log in to the Elementor website with the login details that were sent to your mail when you subscribe for the plan.
- Upon successful login, scroll to the "**my account**" link and click on the **download plugins** link located at the bottom of **"my account"** section to download plugins as a zip file into your desktop.
- Go to your WordPress dashboard and click on **plugins>Add new.** Tap on **upload plugins** at the top of the page and select the zip file you downloaded. Click on the **install** link and then activate the Elementor Pro.
- You will get a prompt at the top of your dashboard telling you to activate the license key. You can activate the license key by tapping on **Elementor** from

your WordPress dashboard. Click on the **license** tab and then choose the "**connect & activate**" link at the bottom.

- You will be taken to a screen where you will be able to log in to your account. Select the **connect** link at the bottom of the page to activate the license.

Alternatively, you can integrate the **Elementor Pro** from your WordPress dashboard by tapping on **Elementor** and choosing **Go Pro** at the bottom.

Getting Ready for the Elementor Experience

Elementor is a website builder plugin for WordPress allowing creation of amazing websites in a rather fun way.

Create a New Page for Your Website

- Navigate to the WordPress dashboard, tap on **Pages** and click on "**Add new.**"
- Enter the Elementor website builder by tapping on the "**Edit with Elementor.**"

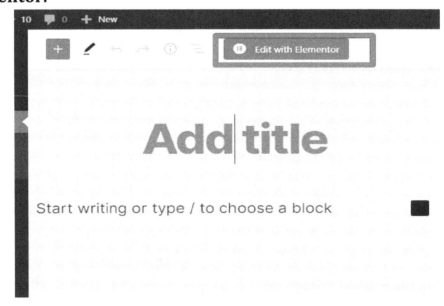

- By clicking on the "**Edit with Elementor,**" you will be taken to the **Elementor panel overview** that looks like the image below;

Elementor #30

Building Your First Page with Elementor

There are three essential building blocks in Elementor, which include; **Sections, Columns** and **Widgets.** The **Columns** sitting inside of **Section** are the ones that house the **Widgets.** This means that **Widgets** are located inside the **Columns.** Each of Section, Column and Widget has different handles, which are used to control them. You can decide to either show or hide the **editing handles** by tapping on the **Elementor hamburger** icon at the top left of the screen to have access to the **Style & Settings** menu. Tap on **user preferences,** scroll down and toggle on the **editing handle** to **Yes.** This will keep showing the editing handles when you are on sections, columns or widget.

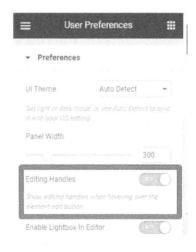

71

Creating Section

- You can create a section by tapping on the ⊕ inside the **drag widget here** box or tap on the ⬤ to make use of a pre-designed page from the Elementor library.
- You will be prompted with the **"Select your structure"** screen where you will be able to choose which structure of section you want.

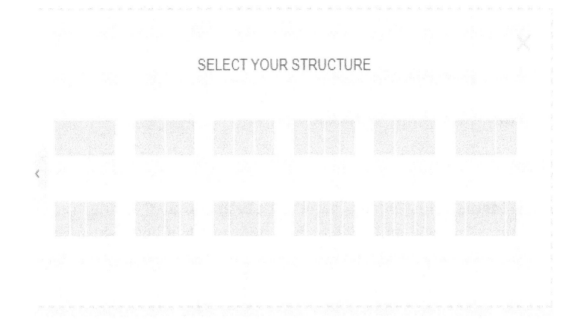

- Use the **section handle** to; **edit** a section, **add** a section and **delete** a section.

To edit a section and choose proper layouts for the section, follow the steps below;

- On the **section handle** , hover your cursor over the **edit section** icon and then right click on it with your mouse.
- You will be prompted with the **edit section** panel at the left side of the screen. The **edit section** panel will allow you to set layout for your section. See below;

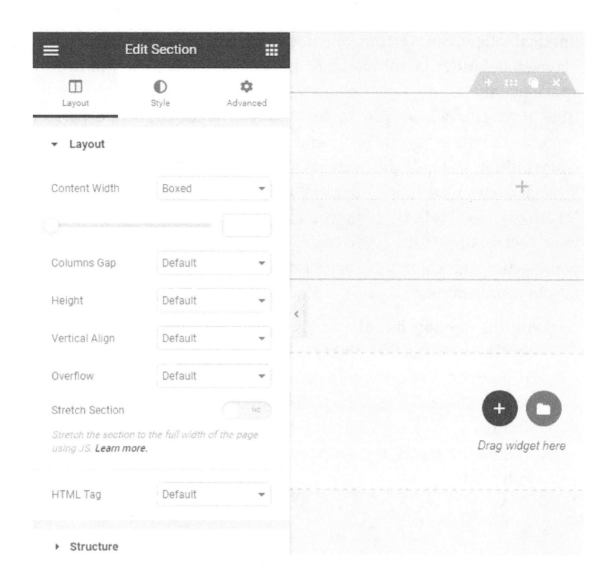

Layout

- **Content width:** Set the width for the content inside the section. You can select between **Full width** and **boxed**. If you chose boxed, utilize the width slider to adjust the width.
- **Column gap:** You can set your column gap and choose between **no gap, narrow, extended, default, wide and wider.**
- **Height:** set the height and tap on the dropdown to select between **default, fit to screen** and **min height.** Choosing **fit to screen** will fit your section to screen.

- **Vertical align:** Set vertical alignment for your section. You can choose between **default, top, middle, bottom, space between, space around and space evenly.**
- **Overflow:** This allows you to set how you want to handle part of your contents that flow beyond its bound. **Default** mode will allow the overflow while **hidden** will hide the contents that overflow.
- **Stretch section:** Stretch the section to the full width of the page.
- **HTML tag:** Set HTML tag for section. To improve your website SEO (making your contents come up at the top of search engines), adding HTML tags to your section and column is very essential. See below for how to add HTML tags in your contents;

  o On the **section handle**, hover your cursor over the **edit section** icon and then right click on it with your mouse.
  o You will be prompted with the **edit section** panel at the left side of the screen. The **edit section** panel will allow you to set layout for your section.
  o Tap on the **HTML tag** dropdown under layout and select the tag that you need

The functions of the respective HTML tags include;

- *<div>* - Use for defining a section in a document

- *<header>* - Use to define a header for a document or section. This is especially important when you are making a header template with Elementor Pro.
- *<footer>* - Use to define a footer for a section or document.
- *<article>* - Use to define an article
- *<section>* - just like *<div>* , it is use for defining a section in a document
- *<aside>* - Use to define content apart from the page content
- *<nav>* - Use to define navigation links.

Style

- **Background:** Choose between **normal** and **hover.** Choosing any of these will allow you to set the background image for your contents.
  - o **Normal background type:** Choose between classic, gradient, video and slideshow.
  - o **Hover background type:** Choose between classic and gradient.

You can then proceed to add background image by tapping on classic, gradient, video or slideshow and then click on the + sign under image to insert image from your computer or WordPress media library.

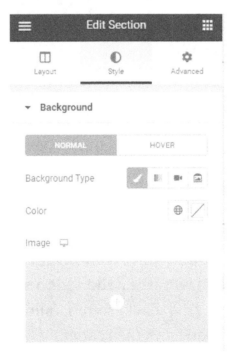

Add the image background color by tapping on the color picker. This will allow you to choose between the default color and setting custom color. When you choose the custom color option, you can begin to tap on the color picker to see how the background in the content area on the right hand side is changing.

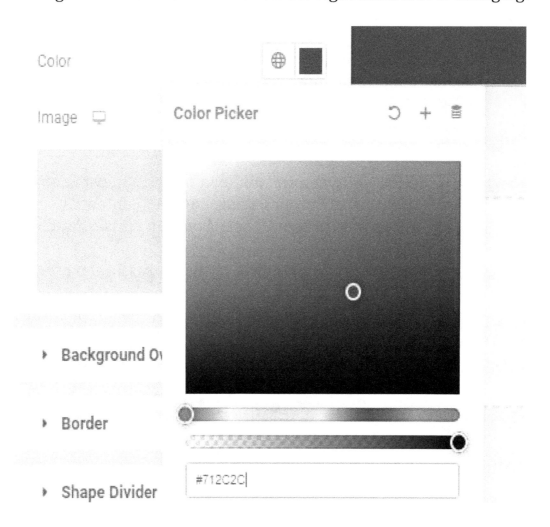

If you choose **video** as your background type, your content background will start showing video and this is what readers will see while reading the content on your website. There is a box where you can paste the video link (either from YouTube or from any other video platforms) that you want to use for the background. You will also be able to set the **video start time, video end time (seconds), whether the video should play once, whether the video should play on mobile and set the background fallback (**the background fallback will be the display image when the video could not load from the readers' end).

- **Background Overlay:** Choose between **normal** and **hover.** Choosing any of these will allow you to set background overlay for your contents. You can select between **classic** and **gradient.** You can also set a blend mode.
- **Border (Normal & Hover)**
  - o **Border Type**: Set a Border Type and choose between **none, solid, double, dotted, dashed and Groove.** See how each of these affects your content's border on the middle section before you finally choose the one you prefer.

- o **Border Radius**: Set your Border Radius. Set the top, right, bottom and left value using the box below the border radius. Also, tap on the desktop icon to set the border radius for the desktop mode, mobile mode and tablet mode.
- o **Box Shadow**: Set a Box Shadow. Use the pencil icon in front of the border shadow to set the horizontal, vertical, blur, spread and position border shadow. Drag the slider to increase or decrease the border shadow.

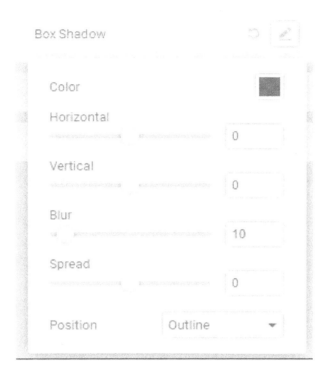

Shape Divider (Top & Bottom): These are shapes that divide/separate the section of a page.

1. **Type**: Tap on the dropdown menu to select your Shape Divider style. You can choose between drop, triangle, zigzag, cloud, curves, arrow etc.

2. **Color**: Select a suitable color

3. **Width**: Choose and adjust the width of the Shape Divider

4. **Height**: Choose and adjust the height of the Shape Divider

5. **Flip**: Flip the Shape divider's direction.

6. **Bring to Front**: Let your Shape Divider be in the front of other objects.

Typography

1. Set the Typography Colors for your section. If you allow default colors, the "set typography" color will not work. You will be able to choose **heading color, text color, link color, link over color and** select how you want your text to be aligned (whether left, right or center).

Advanced: Contains;

Advanced

1. **Margin**: Set margin for your section and choose if this margin should be set for desktop, mobile or tablet.

2. **Padding**: Set the padding for your section and choose if this padding should be set for desktop, mobile or tablet.

3. **Z-index**: Set the Z-Index and choose if this should be set for desktop, mobile or tablet.

4. **CSS ID**: Set a CSS ID for the section

5. **CSS Classes**: Set a CSS Classes for the section

Motion Effects (For Users with Elementor Pro Only)

1. **Sticky**: Set the section as Sticky, and select between Top or Bottom. Setting a sticky header makes your header or menu visible every time. Toggle the **sticky** header to **ON** to set the sticky header.

2. **Scrolling Effects**: Toggle **ON** the scrolling effect to select from an array of animations and interactions that are possible when readers scroll through your page.

3. **Entrance Animation**: Tap on the dropdown to select an animation. You can choose between **Fading, Zooming, Bouncing, Sliding, Rotating, Attention seeker etc.** Tap on the desktop icon to choose whether you are setting for desktop view, mobile view or tablet view.

Responsive

1. **Reverse Columns**: Toggle on the Reverse column (Tablets) to reverse column for tablets and reverse column (mobile) to reverse column for mobile.

2. **Visibility**: You will be able to show or hide the section on mobile, tablet or desktop by toggling on/off the respective switch.

Attributes (for users with Elementor Pro only)

1. Insert your own custom attributes

Column

The **Column** is inside the **section** and has four **editing tools** for the purpose of editing the layout and content inside the column.

- Place your cursor over the edge of the column to have access to; **edit column, duplicate column, add column** and **delete column.**
- You can also right click with your mouse at the edge of the column to have access to these editing tools. When you right click, you will get the editing menus in the image above;
- Add a new column by tapping on the **+ Add new Column** in the image above.

To bring the "**Edit column**" panel, hover the mouse at the edge of the column inside the section and tap on the **edit column** icon. You will see the **edit column** panel at the left hand side of the screen.

Editing Column

Here, you can set column width right under the layout section in the edit column panel. You can also make a lot of settings and adjustments to your column under this section. The Column editing panel has the following menus;

Layout

1. **Column Width (%)**: Set the width for your Columns by using the up and down arrow in the width box. You can also tap on the desktop icon to choose whether you are setting this column for desktop, mobile or tablet view.

2. **Vertical Align**: Set the Column vertical alignment for your contents. By so doing, you will be able to stick the content of all the columns of a certain section to the bottom, the top or the middle or even "stretch to fill" to align the columns with unequal heights. You can select from Top, Bottom, Middle, Space Between, space evenly and Space Around.

3. **Horizontal Align**: This extends the inline positioning capability and allows you to align the inline widgets placed in the same row horizontally. You can select from Start, End, Center, Space Between, space evenly and Space Around.

4. **HTML Tag**: Set HTML tag for section. To improve your website SEO (making your contents come up at the top of search engines), adding HTML tags to your section and column is very essential. See below for how to add HTML tags in your contents;

- o On the **section handle** 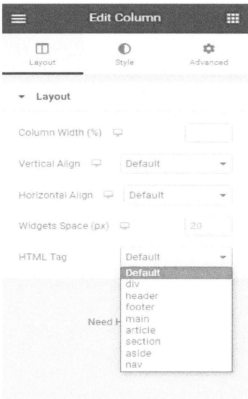, hover your cursor over the **edit section** icon and then right click on it with your mouse.
- o You will be prompted with the **edit section** panel at the left side of the screen. The **edit section** panel will allow you to set layout for your Column.
- o Tap on the **HTML tag** dropdown under layout and select the tag that you need

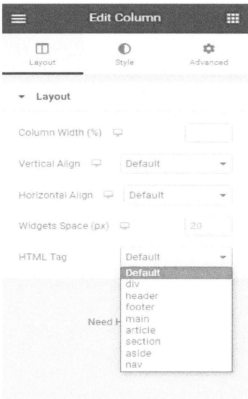

The functions of the respective HTML tags include;

- *<div>* - Use for defining a section in a document

- *<header>* - Use to define a header for a document or section. This is especially important when you are making a header template with Elementor Pro.
- *<footer>* - Use to define a footer for a section or document.
- *<article>* - Use to define an article
- *<section>* - just like *<div>* , it is use for defining a section in a document
- *<aside>* - Use to define content apart from the page content
- *<nav>* - Use to define navigation links.

Style

- **Background:** Choose between **normal** and **hover.** Choosing any of these will allow you to set the background image for the contents inside your column.
  - o **Normal background type:** Choose between classic, gradient and slideshow.
  - o **Hover background type:** Choose between classic and gradient. You will also be able to set transition duration by dragging the transition duration slider to either increase or decrease the duration.

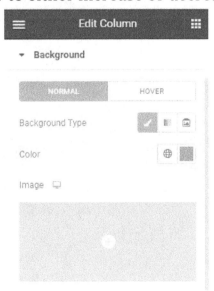

You can then proceed to add background image by tapping on classic, gradient or slideshow and then click on the + sign under image to insert image from your computer or WordPress media library.

Add the image background color by tapping on the color picker. This will allow you to choose between the default color and setting custom color. When you choose the custom color option, you can begin to tap on the color picker to see how the background in the column's content area on the right hand side is changing.

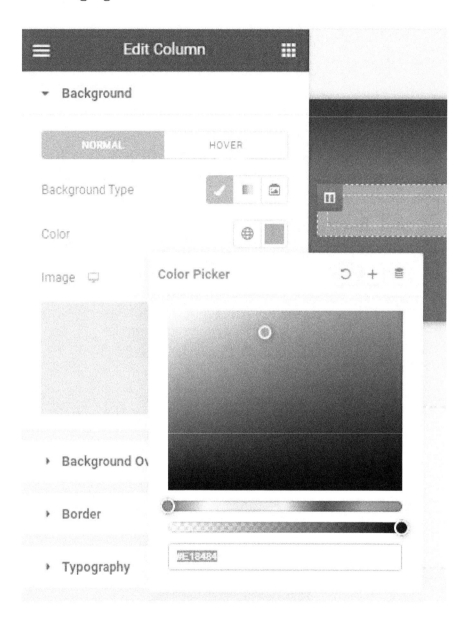

- **Background Overlay (normal and hover):** Choose between **normal** and **hover.** Choosing any of these will allow you to set background overlay for your contents. You can select between **classic** and **gradient.** You can also set a blend mode and the CSS Filter.

- **Border (Normal & Hover)**
  - o **Border Type**: Set a Border Type and choose between **none, solid, double, dotted, dashed and Groove.** See how each of these affects your content's border on the middle section before you finally choose the one you prefer.
  - o **Border Radius**: Set your Border Radius. Set the top, right, bottom and left value using the box below the border radius. Also, tap on the desktop icon to set the border radius for the desktop mode, mobile mode and tablet mode.
  - o **Box Shadow**: Set a Box Shadow. Use the pencil icon in front of the border shadow to set the horizontal, vertical, blur, spread and position border shadow. Drag the slider to increase or decrease the border shadow.

- **Typography**

Set the Typography Colors for your column. If you allow default colors, the "set typography" color will not work. You will be able to choose **heading color, text color, link color, link over color and** select how you want your text to be aligned (whether left, right or center).

Advanced: Contains;

Advanced

- **Margin**: Set margin for your section and choose if this margin should be set for desktop, mobile or tablet.
- **Padding**: Set the padding for your section and choose if this padding should be set for desktop, mobile or tablet.
- **Z-index**: Set the Z-Index and choose if this should be set for desktop, mobile or tablet. The Z-Index is used to indicate the stack order for an element. An element with a higher stack order will normally be in the front of an element with a smaller stack order.
- **CSS ID**: Set a CSS ID for the section
- **CSS Classes**: Set a CSS Classes for the section

Motion Effects (for users with Elementor Pro only)

- **Sticky**: Set the section as Sticky, and select between Top or Bottom. Setting a sticky header makes your header or menu visible every time. Toggle the **sticky** header to **ON** to set the sticky header.
- **Scrolling Effects**: Toggle **ON** the scrolling effect to select from an array of animations and interactions that are possible when readers scroll through your page.
- **Entrance Animation**: Tap on the dropdown to select an animation. You can choose between **Fading, Zooming, Bouncing, Sliding, Rotating, Attention seeker etc.** Tap on the desktop icon to choose whether you are setting for desktop view, mobile view or tablet view.

Responsive

- **Reverse Columns**: Toggle on the Reverse column (Tablets) to reverse column for tablets and reverse column (mobile) to reverse column for mobile.
- **Visibility**: You will be able to show or hide the section on mobile, tablet or desktop by toggling on/off the respective switch.

Attributes (for users with Elementor Pro only)

1. Insert your own custom attributes

Widgets

Place widgets inside the column. Drag and then drop any widget - from the left navigation pane of the Elementor dashboard – in the widget area inside the column box. There are many categories of widgets that you can add;

Button Widget

This widget allows users to design and customize buttons without necessarily downloading any button plugins in WordPress. To use the button widget, drag and drop the button widget from the left side of the Elementor panel inside the column (widget are positioned inside the column). The **Button widget** editing tools 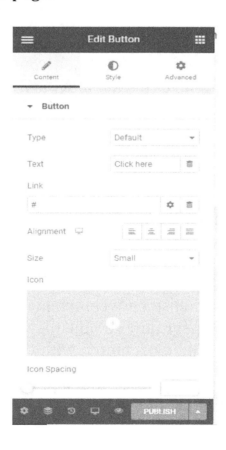 located at the right edge of the widget box can be used to edit various widget settings. Right click on the **edit widget** icon from one of the three widget tools and you will have the **edit panel** for any widget you dropped inside the widget box. Since we are working on the button widget, you will have the **"Edit button"** panel at the left navigation pane of the Elementor dashboard.

Note: When you are browsing a web page, you will most likely come across a **"click here"** link that will either take you down the page or open the link in another window on your browser. This type of link is usually created using the **button widget.** The **"click here"** in the button widget can usually be edited and another text can be written inside. The text will be clickable and will take readers to a new page or down the page.

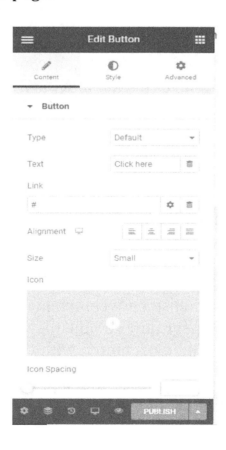

- **Content**
    - o **Type:** You can choose between five types of widget buttons including **default, info, success, warning** and **danger.** When you select one of

these button types, you will see the [Click here] link at the left side of the button widget box changing color depending on which button type was selected. A warning widget button type will usually have a red color.

- o **Text:** Enter the text for the button. This text will replace the "**Click here**" text. You will see the **"Click here"** immediately changing into the text you are entering here.

- o **Link:** You will be able to add a link to the button. This link will be hidden in the button widget and the reader will only see the link once they open the "**Click here**" and another window is opened. Also, tap on the **setting** icon below link to set the link option. The link option can be set to; **open in new window** and **add no follow.** When you tap on the **open in new window,** the link will open for the user in a new window.

- o **Alignment:** You will be able to align the button widget to either the right, left, center and justified. When you tap on the right align, you will see the "**Click here**" button moving from left (if it was initially at the left) to the right hand side of the Widget box.

- o **Size:** Choose the size for the button widget. You can choose between Extra small, small, medium, large and extra-large.

- o **Icon spacing:** Drag the icon spacing slider forward or backward to choose the spacing for the "**click here**" icon. Dragging it forward will increase the icon spacing and dragging it backward will decrease the icon spacing.

- **Style**
  - o **Typography**: This allows you to change the way the text of the button appears. You can choose between many text fonts. Tap on the pencil icon in front or typography to edit the typography options for your button, and you will be prompted with the typography menus where you can change text fonts (**family),** size of texts and how texts will appear on; desktop, mobile and tablets, text weight (allows you to set the thickness of texts), transform (allows you to set whether you want your texts in upper case, lower case, capitalize first letters or default mode), decoration (allows you to choose whether you want to underline your text, Overline your text by placing a line above the text

or line through the text), line height (adjust the height of the text icon with the height slider) and letter spacing.

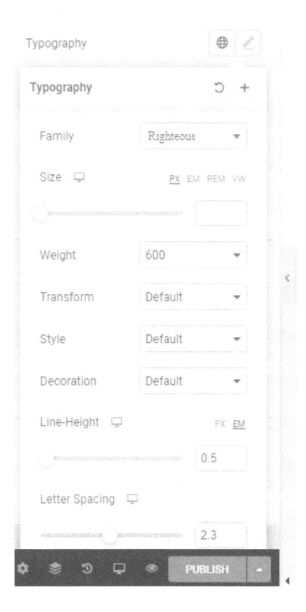

- ○ **Text Shadow**: Insert a shadow and blur to the text's button.
- ○ **Text Color**: Choose the button's text color.
- ○ **Background Color**: Choose background color for the button in both the normal and hover modes.
- ○ **Hover Animation**: Set a hover animation by tapping on the **hover** tab. You can choose between pop, grow, shrink, pulse, push etc.
- ○ **Border Type**: Choose the border type to use around the button.

- o **Width**: Control the border's thickness around the button. You can adjust the top, right, bottom and left thickness for the border around the button.
- o **Color**: Pick a color for the border with a color picker.
- o **Border Radius**: Set the radius for the border to control corner roundness
- o **Box Shadow**: Tap on the pencil icon in front of the box shadow to set a shadow for the box that contains the button's text. You can set the shadow for horizontal, vertical, spread and blur.
- o **Padding**: Change the button's padding settings.

- **Advanced:** Contains;

Advanced

- **Margin**: Set margin for your section and choose if this margin should be set for desktop, mobile or tablet.
- **Padding**: Set the padding for your section and choose if this padding should be set for desktop, mobile or tablet.
- **Z-index**: Set the Z-Index and choose if this should be set for desktop, mobile or tablet. The Z-Index is used to indicate the stack order for an element. An element with a higher stack order will normally be in the front of an element with a smaller stack order.
- **CSS ID**: Set a CSS ID for the section
- **CSS Classes**: Set a CSS Classes for the section.

Motion Effects (for users with Elementor Pro only)

- **Sticky**: Set the section as Sticky, and select between Top or Bottom. Setting a sticky header makes your header or menu visible every time. Toggle the **sticky** header to **ON** to set the sticky header.
- **Scrolling Effects**: Toggle **ON** the scrolling effect to select from an array of animations and interactions that are possible when readers scroll through your page.
- **Entrance Animation**: Tap on the dropdown to select an animation. You can choose between **Fading, Zooming, Bouncing, Sliding, Rotating, Attention**

seeker etc. Tap on the desktop icon to choose whether you are setting for desktop view, mobile view or tablet view.

Responsive

- **Reverse Columns**: Toggle on the Reverse column (Tablets) to reverse column for tablets and reverse column (mobile) to reverse column for mobile.
- **Visibility**: You will be able to show or hide the section on mobile, tablet or desktop by toggling on/off the respective switch.

Attributes (for users with Elementor Pro only)

- Insert your own custom attributes

- **Positioning**

1. **Width:** Choose the width of the element. You can choose from Full width (100%), custom or Inline (auto) width.

2. **Custom Width**: This will only show if you selected the **custom** under the width section. You will be able to use the width slider to customize the width you want for the element. You can also tap on the desktop icon to choose if this setting is only applicable to desktop user, mobile or tablet users.

3. **Vertical Align**: This will only show if you selected **Full width** or **Inline** under the Width section. You can also choose to show the element at the start, middle (center) or at the end.

4. **Position**: Choose the position of the element, select either Default, Absolute, Fixed, or Custom. The **Absolute** option will position an element absolutely to its first positioned parent. The **Fixed** option will position an element relative to the user's viewport.

If you select either Absolute or Fixed, you will have access to the following options;

1. **Horizontal Orientation**: Choose either **start** or **end** to set a horizontal reference point for the absolute positioning.

2. **Offset**: Use the offset slider to adjust the horizontal reference point by the amount of the offset.

3. **Vertical Orientation**: Choose either **start** or **end** to set a vertical reference point for the absolute positioning.

4. **Offset**: Use the offset slider to adjust the vertical reference point by the amount of the offset.

CHAPTER FIVE

THE TEXT EDITOR WIDGET

The Text Editor Widget, just like the visual classic editor or any other type of Editor in WordPress, allows you to enter texts, images and some WordPress Shortcodes. The Text Editor widget provides better styling options in texts more than the Classic Editor in WordPress; as it allows you to change settings like line height, font weight, letter spacing etc.

To start using the Text Editor Widget, simply drag it from the list of widgets at the left hand side of the Elementor dashboard and drop inside the column on the right hand side. Once you drag and drop the text editor widget, you will see the text editor panel below on the left hand side

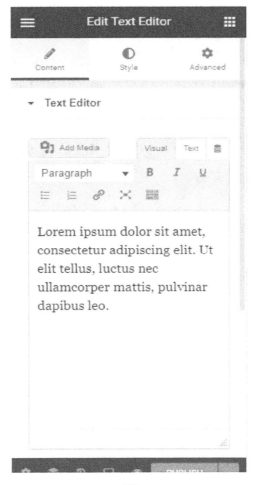

Content

You can begin to type your content inside the content area above and you can see the texts changing inside the widget on the right hand side. See below;

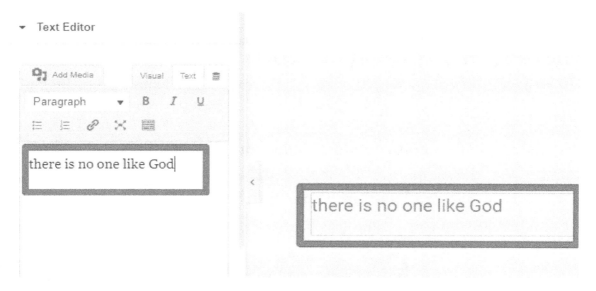

The Text Editor panel has a number of features that can allow you to properly style your contents and provide the needed aesthetic for your writings.

Scroll down to the bottom of the content section and **toggle on** the **Drop Cap** to set the first letter of your text as **large** as possible which makes it unique from other parts of the text. See below;

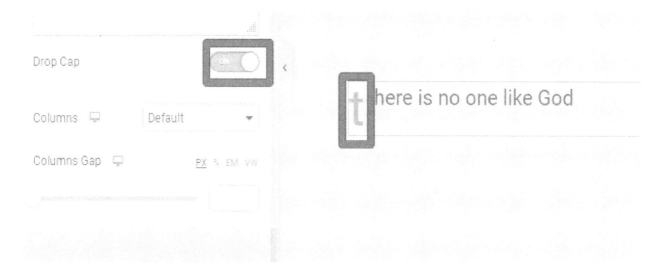

Use the columns drop down to set how many columns you want your texts to be divided into. You can choose the default column or set the column between 1 and 10. Setting the column to 10 will look exactly like the image below;

Style

Text Editor

1. **Alignment**: Use the alignment option to set and align your text to the left, center, right or justified. Tapping on the right alignment will shift your texts to the right hand side while the center will shift texts to the center.

2. **Text Color**: Pick the text's color. Tap on the color picker beside the text color to bring a color wheel. Start tapping inside the color wheel to see how the text inside the text editor widget is changing.

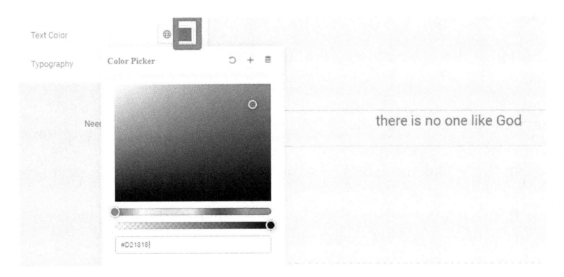

3. **Typography**: Tap on the pencil like beside typography and you can see the following setting options;

1. **Family**: Choose the text family here. There are many text's variants you can choose from here. Once you select a text variant, use the size slider to adjust the size of the text.

2. **Weight**: Allows you to choose the weight of the text. This signifies how thick the text will be. Choose a value by using the dropdown.

3. **Transform:** Transform your texts into UPPERCASE (changes all text into upper case), lowercase (changes all texts into lower case), Capitalize (capitalizes all initials) and default.

4. **Style:** Choose between *italicize (*italicize texts), oblique, normal and default.

5. **Line height:** Select a value for the height of the widget line

6. **Letter spacing:** Select a value to adjust spaces between letters of your texts.

4. **Columns**: Set the number of columns you want to split your text into

5. **Column Gap**: Select the width of the gap between columns

Drop Cap

1. **View**: Choose the view style of the drop cap, select from Default, Framed or Stacked.

2. **Primary Color**: Select the color of the drop cap

3. **Space**: Set the actual space between the drop cap and the other part of the text

4. **Border Radius**: If you selected Stacked or Framed as the View, set your border radius to control and adjust corner roundness

5. **Typography**: Set typography options for the drop cap

Advanced: Contains;

- **Advanced**
    - **Margin**: Set margin for the content inside the text editor widget and choose if this margin should be set for desktop, mobile or tablet. Use the up and down arrow to choose a value and you can see how the texts in the editor is changing margin
    - **Padding**: Set the padding for the content inside the text editor and choose if this padding should be set for desktop, mobile or tablet. Use the up and down arrow to choose a value and you can see how the texts in the editor are changing. See image below;

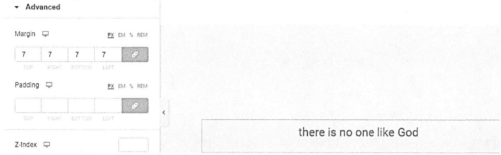

    - **Z-index**: Set the Z-Index and choose if this should be set for desktop, mobile or tablet. The Z-Index is used to indicate the stack order for an element. An element with a higher stack order will normally be in the front of an element with a smaller stack order.
    - **CSS ID**: Set a CSS ID for the section
    - **CSS Classes**: Set a CSS Classes for the section.

Motion Effects

- **Entrance Animation**: Tap on the dropdown to select an animation. You can choose between **Fading, Zooming, Bouncing, Sliding, Rotating, Attention seeker etc.** Tap on the desktop icon to choose whether you are setting for desktop view, mobile view or tablet view. Setting animation will make your texts start moving in any direction depending on which animation you choose. For instance, you can experiment with the **Fading** animation and select **Fade In Up.** The Fade In Up will allow you to set animation duration (as either fast or slow) and also set the time for the animation delay. Once you enter all the required details, you will see the texts in the editor widget moving up (with animation).

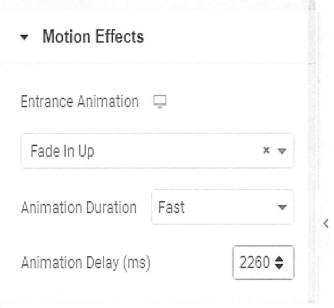

Responsive

- **Visibility**: You will be able to show or hide the section on mobile, tablet or desktop by toggling on/off the respective switch. Responsive visibility will take effect only on the live website or the preview page and not while editing in Elementor.

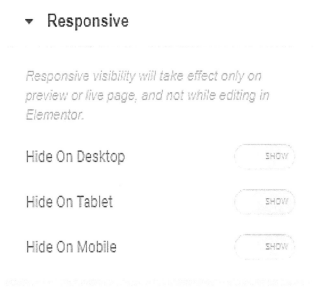

Attributes (for users with Elementor Pro only)

2. Insert your own HTML custom attributes to every element. You need to get the Elementor Pro version to do this.

Positioning

5. **Width:** Choose the width of the element. You can choose from Full width (100%), custom or Inline (auto) width.

6. **Custom Width**: This will only show if you selected the **custom** under the width section. You will be able to use the width slider to customize the width you want for the element. You can also tap on the desktop icon to choose if this setting is only applicable to desktop users, mobile or tablet users.

   Note: Custom positioning is not considered best practice for responsive web design and should not be used too frequently.

7. **Vertical Align**: This will only show if you selected **Full width** or **Inline** under the Width section. You can also choose to show the element at the start, middle (center) or at the end.

8. **Position**: Choose the position of the element, select either Default, Absolute, Fixed, or Custom. The **Absolute** option will position an element absolutely to its first positioned parent. The **Fixed** option will position an element relative to the user's viewport.

   If you select either Absolute or Fixed, you will have access to the following options;

5. **Horizontal Orientation**: Choose either **top** or **bottom** to set a horizontal reference point for the absolute positioning.

6. **Offset**: Use the offset slider to adjust the horizontal reference point by the amount of the offset.

7. **Vertical Orientation**: Choose either **top** or **bottom** to set a vertical reference point for the absolute positioning.

8. **Offset**: Use the offset slider to adjust the vertical reference point by the amount of the offset

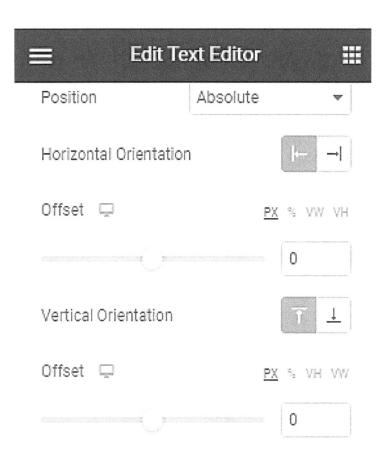

How to Wrap Text Around Images With the Text Editor Widget

To wrap text around images in Elementor using the text editor widget, follow the steps below;

✓ Drag in the **text editor** widget.

✓ Tap on **add media** and you will be taken to the media library where you can either select a picture from your computer or use one from the media library.

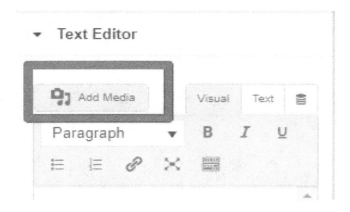

✓ Tap on **add media** and the image will be inserted inside the text editor panel and at the right hand side (inside the text editor widget containing your texts)

✓ Tap on the image inside the text editor panel and you will see the **image alignment** options. See below;

✓ Use any of the adjustment tools to wrap the image to the right of texts or to the left of texts. You can even wrap the image anywhere around texts. See the result below;

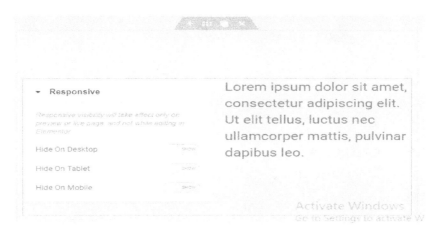

Text Editor Widget doesn't have the text tab and the visual tab?

It is possible that you have disabled the visual editor in WordPress settings, and to enable the visual editor you need to follow the prompts below;

- Navigate to the WordPress dashboard, scroll down and tap on **Users**

- Select **profile** and you will be taken to your profile section

- Uncheck the "**Disable the visual editor when writing**" box

- Scroll down the page and tap on **"Update profile"** to save the change.

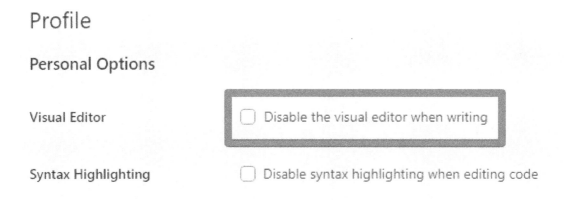

The Icon Widget

Use the icon widget to show beautiful icons in many styles on your page.

The Icon Widget panel has three different views all of which come with different settings. You can choose between **Default view, Stacked View** and **Framed view.**

If you selected the **default view,** you can have access to the following menus;

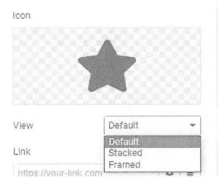

Content

1. **Icon**: Tap on the icon image to choose from a list of icons or upload SVG. Place your cursor over the icon image, select **icon library** and you will be taken to the icon library where you can choose any icon type that you want.

The icon library is as shown below. Select any icon type that you want and tap on **insert** at the bottom of the screen.

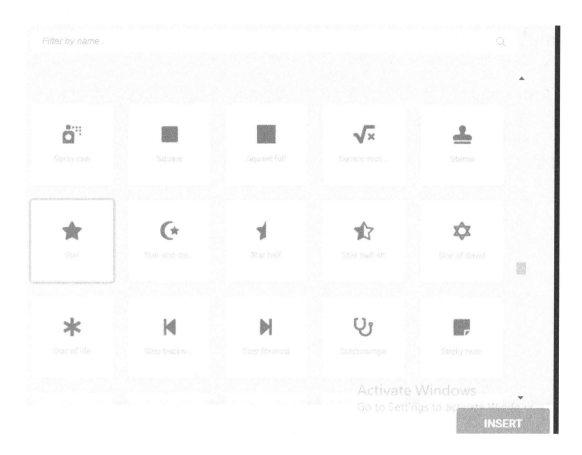

2. **View**: Select between default, Framed or stacked.

3. **Link**: Input the URL for the icon. Once users click on the icon, they will be directed to this link for them to access the information contained in there. Tap on the **link options** ✿ to choose between **open the link in a new window** (this will open new window once users tap on the icon) and **add nofollow** (don't open in new window)

4. **Alignment**: Use the alignment tab to set icons to the right, left or center. You can also choose whether this setting is applicable only on desktop, tablet or mobile.

Style

Icon

Normal

104

1. **Primary**: Tap on the color picker to select color for the icon. The color wheel will be displayed and you can start tapping inside the color wheel to see how the widget is changing color.

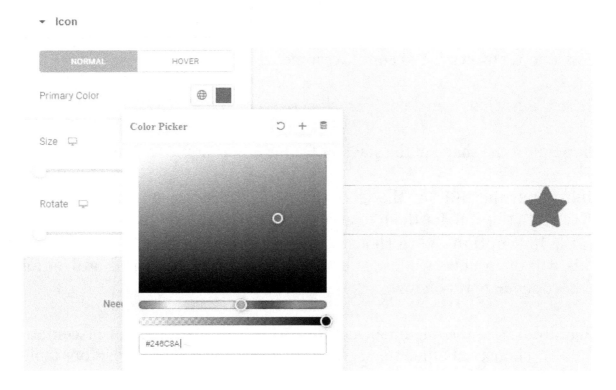

2. **Size**: Use the size slider to drag forward (Increase) or drag backward (decrease) the size of the icon.

3. **Rotate**: Drag the slider to rotate the icon

Hover

1. **Primary Color**: Tap on the color picker to select color for the icon in the hover state. The color wheel will be displayed and you can start tapping inside the color wheel to see how the widget is changing color.

2. **Hover Animation**: Set animation for the hover state

3. **Size**: Use the size slider to choose the icon size.

4. **Rotate**: You will be able to rotate the icon up to 360 degrees.

If **Stacked** or **Framed** view is chosen, the following options are available:

Content

1. **Icon**: Choose from a list of Font Awesome icons

2. **View**: Choose between default, stacked or framed

3. **Shape**: Pick the shape of the stack or frame, either Circle or Square

4. **Link**: Input the URL for the icon. Once users click on the icon, they will be directed to this link for them to access the information contained in there. Tap on the **link options** ✿ to choose between **open the link in a new window** (this will open new window once users tap on the icon) and **add nofollow** (don't open in new window

5. **Alignment**: Use the alignment tab to set icons to the right, left or center. You can also choose whether this setting is applicable only on desktop, tablet or mobile.

Style

Icon

Normal

1. **Primary Color**: Select the primary (the background or frame) color for your icon

2. **Secondary Color**: Select the secondary color, which is the icon's color itself

3. **Padding**: Control the size of the stack or frame by setting the padding around the icon.

4. **Size**: Use the size slider to set the icon's size.

5. **Rotate**: You will be able to rotate the icon up to 360 degrees.

6. **Border Radius**: Control the corner roundness of the frame or stack by setting a specific border radius

Hover

1. **Primary Color**: Choose the primary color (the background or frame) color for the icon

2. **Secondary Color**: Select the secondary color, which is the icon's color itself.

3. **Hover Animation**: Pick an animation effect when moving over the icon. Select from Grow, Pulse, Skew, etc.

4. **Padding**: Control the size of the stack or frame by setting the padding around the icon.

5. **Size**: Use the size slider to set the icon's size.

6. **Rotate**: You will be able to rotate the icon up to 360 degrees.

7. **Border Radius**: Control the corner roundness of the frame or stack by setting a specific border radius.

The Icon List Widget

Use the icon list widget to create an easy to follow list of items. Each item will be highlighted by its own icon.

To have access to the **Edit Icon list,** drag and drop the **icon list widget** into the widget space at the right hand side. The Edit icon list is as shown below;

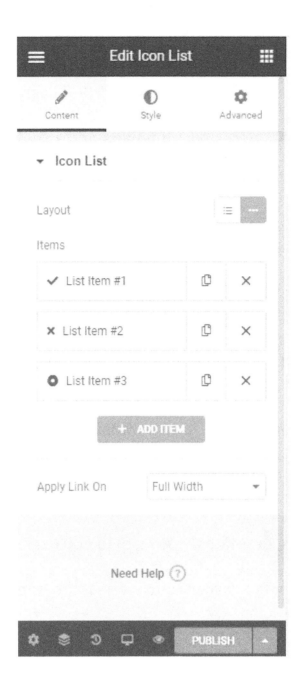

Content tab

- **Icon list:** Contains;

    ○ **Layout:** Choose between **default** and **inline.** The **default** ≡ mode will arrange your items in a vertical list while the **inline** ⠿ mode will arrange your items in a horizontal list.

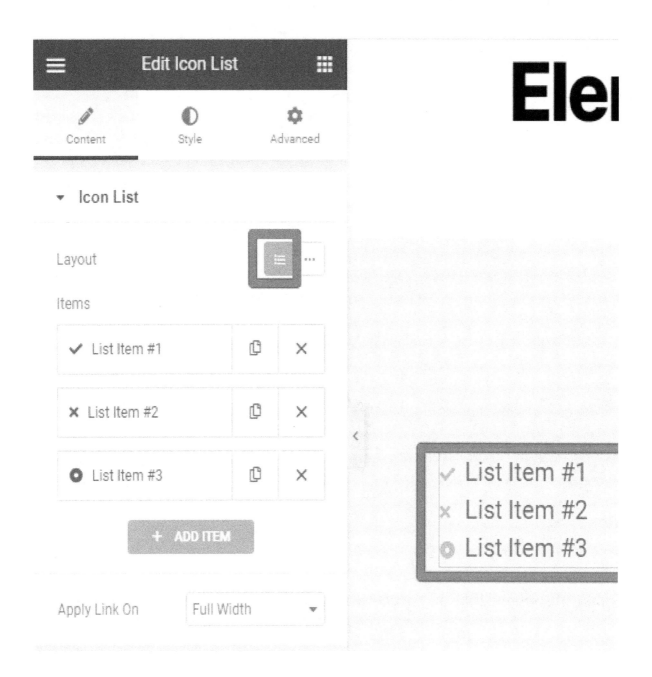

- ○ **Items**
- ○ **Text:** Tap on List item#1 to bring the;
- ▪ **text box (**where you can enter the text you want to replace the list item#1).
- ▪ **icon (**to display the list of icons you can choose from the icon library) and;
- ▪ **link (**to add a link to the icon). Tap on the link option setting to set whether the link you add to the icon should open in a new window or not.

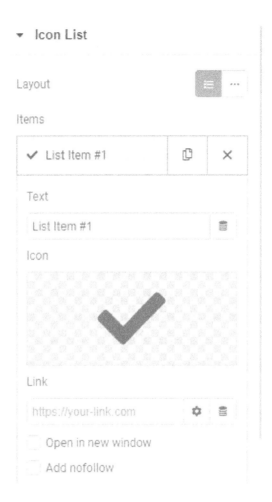

Style

List

1. **Space Between**: Use the **space between** sliders to adjust space between list items.

2. **Alignment**: Use the alignment option to align the list item to the left, right, or center.

3. **Divider**: Tap on the divider switch to turn it on/off. When you turn on the divider line, you will get the following menus;

   - **Style**: Tap on the box beside the **style** to select between solid, dotted, double or dashed.

- **Weight**: Use the width slider to set the thickness of the divider

- **Width**: Control the divider's width relative to the container

- **Color**: Select color for the divider.

Icon

1. **Color**: Bring the color wheel and select color for the icon list. Keep tapping inside the color wheel to pick a suitable color for the icon list.

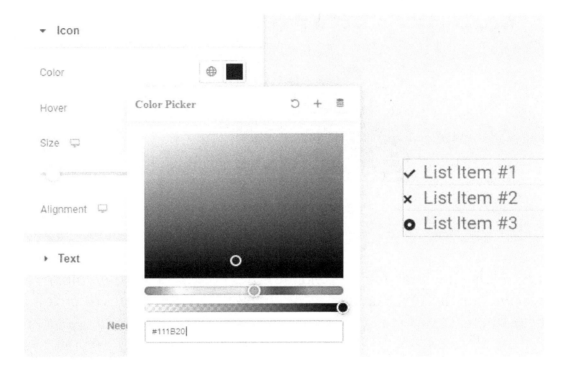

2. **Hover**: Select the color for the icon in hover state. Bring the color wheel and select color for the icon list. Keep tapping inside the color wheel to pick a suitable color for the icon list.

3. **Size**: Use the size slider to set the size of the icon. Drag forward to increase the icon size and drag backward to reduce the icon size.

4. **Alignment**: Use the alignment option to align the icon to the left, right, or center.

Text

1. **Text Color**: Tap on the color picker to choose the color for your texts. Bring the color wheel and select color for the text. Keep tapping inside the color wheel to pick a suitable color for the text.

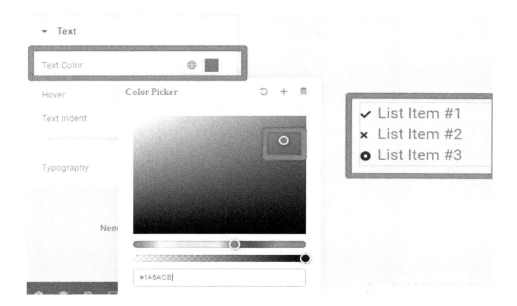

2. **Hover**: Select the color for the text in hover state. Bring the color wheel and select color for the text. Keep tapping inside the color wheel to pick a suitable color for the text.

3. **Text Indent**: Set the distance between the text and the icon by using the text indent slider.

4. **Typography**: Tap on the pencil like beside typography and you can see the following setting options;

- **Family**: Choose the text family here. There are many text's variants you can choose from here. Once you select a text variant, use the size slider to adjust the size of the text inside the icon list widget.

- **Weight**: Allows you to choose the weight of the text. This signifies how thick the text will be. Choose a value by using the dropdown.

- **Transform:** Transform your texts into UPPERCASE (changes all text into upper case), lowercase (changes all texts into lower case), Capitalize (capitalizes all initials) and default.

- **Style:** Choose between *italicize* (italicize texts), oblique, normal and default.

- **Line height:** Select a value for the height of the widget line

- **Letter spacing:** Select a value to adjust spaces between letters of your texts.

Advanced: The Advanced settings applicable to this widget include;

- **Advanced**
  - **Margin**: Set margin for the content inside the icon list widget and choose if this margin should be set for desktop, mobile or tablet. Use the up and down arrow to choose a value and you can see how the texts in the editor is changing margin
  - **Padding**: Set the padding for the content inside the icon list widget and choose if this padding should be set for desktop, mobile or tablet. Use the up and down arrow to choose a value and you can see how the texts in the editor are changing. See image below;

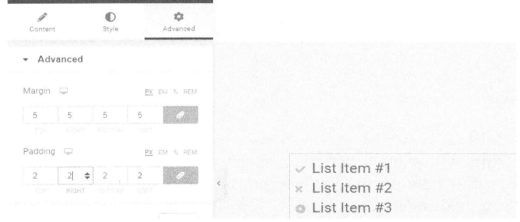

- **Z-index**: Set the Z-Index and choose if this should be set for desktop, mobile or tablet. The Z-Index is used to indicate the stack order for an element. An element with a higher stack order will normally be in the front of an element with a smaller stack order.
- **CSS ID**: Set a CSS ID for the section
- **CSS Classes**: Set a CSS Classes for the section.

Motion Effects

- **Entrance Animation**: Tap on the dropdown to select an animation. You can choose between **Fading, Zooming, Bouncing, Sliding, Rotating, Attention seeker etc.** Tap on the desktop icon to choose whether you are setting for desktop view, mobile view or tablet view. Setting animation will make your texts start moving in any direction depending on which animation you choose. For instance, you can experiment with the **Fading** animation and select **Fade In Up.** The Fade In Up will allow you to set animation duration (as either fast or slow) and also set the time for the animation delay. Once you enter all the required details, you will see the texts in the editor widget moving up (with animation).

Responsive

- **Visibility**: You will be able to show or hide the section on mobile, tablet or desktop by toggling on/off the respective switch. Responsive visibility will take effect only on the live website or the preview page and not while editing in Elementor.

Attributes (for users with Elementor Pro only)

3. Insert your own HTML custom attributes to every element. You need to get the Elementor Pro version to do this.

Positioning

- **Width:** Choose the width of the element. You can choose from Full width (100%), custom or Inline (auto) width.
- **Custom Width**: This will only show if you selected the **custom** under the width section. You will be able to use the width slider to customize the width you want for the element. You can also tap on the desktop icon to choose if this setting is only applicable to desktop user, mobile or tablet users.

Note: Custom positioning is not considered best practice for responsive web design and should not be used too frequently.

- **Vertical Align**: This will only show if you selected **Full width** or **Inline** under the Width section. You can also choose to show the element at the start, middle (center) or at the end.

- **Position**: Choose the position of the element, select either Default, Absolute, Fixed, or Custom. The **Absolute** option will position an element absolutely to its first positioned parent. The **Fixed** option will position an element relative to the user's viewport.

If you select either Absolute or Fixed, you will have access to the following options;

- **Horizontal Orientation**: Choose either **right** or **left** to set a horizontal reference point for the absolute positioning.
- **Offset**: Use the offset slider to adjust the horizontal reference point by the amount of the offset.
- **Vertical Orientation**: Choose either **right** or **left** to set a vertical reference point for the absolute positioning.
- **Offset**: Use the offset slider to adjust the vertical reference point by the amount of the offset.

The Call to Action Widget (CTA)

Deploy a CTA widget to show visitors what to do. This widget has a title, subtitle and a button. It is a simple way to call users to actions. The following settings are available;

CONTENT

Image;

1. **Skin**: Here, you can select either the Cover skin or the Classic skin.

2. **Layout** (Only available if you chose Classic skin): You will be able to align your image to the right, left, or on top of the image

   If you selected **Classic Skin,** you will have access to the following options;

Content;

1. **Graphic Element**: Show a graphical element by choosing between None, Image or Icon.

2. If you chose image as the Graphic Element:
   Choose Image: Tap on this to select or upload an image
   Image Size: Choose between the available image size (thumbnail to full) or set a custom image size.

3. If you selected icon as the Graphic Element:
   Icon: Choose an icon from the icon library.
   View: Choose between the default icon view, stacked or framed.

4. **Title & Description**: Select the title and description that will show in the front of the flip box

5. **Title HTML Tag**: Set the HTML tag of the title to H1- H6, Div, or Span

6. **Button Text**: Write the text to be shown on the button

7. **Link**: Input the URL for the button's link. Tap on the Link Options cog ⚙ to either choose between **add nofollow** to the link or to **open the link in a new window.**

RIBBON

Title: Write the text you want to show on the ribbon.

STYLE

Box;

1. **Min. Height** - Set minimum height of the whole box

2. **Alignment** – Adjust the content inside the CTA widget to the right, center or left of the box

3. **Vertical Position** – Adjust the content inside the CTA widget to the bottom, top or center of the box.

4. **Padding -** Set the content's padding.

Image;

1. **Min. Width**: Set the image's minimum width.

2. **Min. Height**: Set the image's minimum height.

Content;

Title

1. **Typography**: Assign the typography options for the title. Tap on the pencil like beside typography and you can see the following setting options;

    • **Family**: Choose the text family here. There are many text's variants you can choose from here. Once you select a text variant, use the size slider to adjust the size of the text.

    • **Weight**: Allows you to choose the weight of the text. This signifies how thick the text will be. Choose a value by using the dropdown.

    • **Transform:** Transform your texts into UPPERCASE (changes all text into upper case), lowercase (changes all texts into lower case), Capitalize (capitalizes all initials) and default.

    • **Style:** Choose between *italicize (*italicize texts), oblique, normal and default.

    • **Line height:** Select a value for the height of the widget line

    • **Letter spacing:** Select a value to adjust spaces between letters of your texts.

2. **Spacing**: Adjust the spacing between the description and the title.

Description

1. **Typography**: Set the typography options for the title. The settings here are the same with the title.

2. **Spacing**: Adjust the spacing between the button and the description.

Colors

1. **Background Color**: Pick the color for the background.

2. **Title Color**: Select the color for the title.

3. **Description Color**: Choose the color for the description.

4. **Button Color**: Choose the color for the button.

Button

1. **Size**: Here, you will be able to choose the size for the button.

2. **Text Color**: Pick the color for the text in the button.

3. **Background Color**: Select the color for the background of the button.

4. **Border Color**: Pick a suitable color for the button's border

5. **Border Width**: Set the width for the border.

6. **Border Radius**: Control the corner roundness by setting the border radius.

Ribbon;

1. **Background Color**: Pick a suitable color for the background of the ribbon.

2. **Text Color**: Select a suitable color for the ribbon's text.

3. **Distance**: Set the distance for the ribbon by adjusting the slider.

4. **Typography**: Set ribbon's title typography options.

5. **Box Shadow**: Set the ribbon's box shadow settings.

Hover effects

1. **Sequenced Animation**: Decide if you want the animation for the text elements to appear sequenced or all at once

2. **Hover Animation**: Select the hover animation for the image. Choose between Zoom in or out, or move right, left, up or down.

The following settings can be set independently for both the **hover** and **normal** states;

1. **Overlay Color**: Pick the image overlay color.

2. **CSS Filters**: Adjust blur, contrast, brightness, and saturation for the image.

3. **Blend Mode**: This is available only for Normal state. Tap to set a blend mode

4. **Transition Duration (in microseconds)**: (For Hover state) Set the time duration in microseconds for the hover effect

If you selected **Cover Skin**, you will have access to the following options:

Content

- **Graphic Element**: Show a graphical element by choosing between None, Image or Icon.

  - If you chose image as the Graphic Element:

Choose Image: Tap on this to select or upload an image

Image Size: Choose between the available image size (thumbnail to full) or set a custom image size.

  o If you selected icon as the Graphic Element:

Icon: Choose an icon from the icon library.

View: Choose between the default icon view, stacked or framed.

- **Title & Description**: Select the title and description that will show in the front of the flip box.

- **Title HTML Tag**: Set the HTML tag of the title to H1- H6, Div, or Span.
- **Button Text**: Write the text to be shown on the button
- **Link**: Input the URL for the button's link. Tap on the Link Options cog ⚙ to either choose between **add nofollow** to the link or to **open the link in a new window.**

RIBBON

- **Title**: Enter the text to be displayed on the ribbon.

STYLE;

- **Box**

You will be able to set the **Min. Height, Alignment, vertical position and padding** just like you set them when you chose **Classic Skin.**

CONTENT

- **Title;**

You will be able to set the **Typography and Spacing** just the same way you set them for **Classic Skin.**

- **Colors**

You will be able to set the **Title Color**: and **Button color** just like you set them for **Classic Skin.**

Button

You will be able to set the **Size, Typography, Text color, background color, border color, border width and border radius** just like you set them for the **classic skin.**

Ribbon

You should set the **Background Color, Text color, distance, typography and Box shadow** just like you did for **classic skin.**

HOVER EFFECTS

- **Content**

1. **Hover Animation**: Decide between the choices for the hover animation for your image: you can choose between Zoom in or out, or move left, right, down or up.

2. **Animation Duration**: Assign the length of time it will take the animation to complete

3. **Sequenced Animation**: Decide if the animation for the text elements should appear sequenced or all at once

- **Background**

1. **Hover Animation**: Decide between the choices for the hover animation for your image: you can choose between Zoom in or out, or move left, right, down or up.

2. **Overlay Color**: Select the overlay color for the normal mode and hover mode.

3. **CSS Filters**: Set blur, brightness, contrast and saturation for the image

4. **Blend Mode**: (For Normal state) Choose a blend mode for the image

5. **Transition Duration (ms)**: (For Hover state) Set the duration in microseconds for the hover effect

Adding Templates in Elementor

Templates are just pages and blocks (pre-designed) that you can insert in your pages. To add templates, follow the steps below;

- From the Elementor dashboard, tap on the **add template** icon at the middle section of the page.

- Tap on the **magnifying glass** icon to preview any template you want to use from the list of templates available.
- Tap on the **insert** link at the bottom of the template you want to select.
- Tap on the **upload** arrow at the top right hand corner.

PREVIEWING AND PUBLISHING YOUR PAGE

Once you have successfully designed your page, the next thing is to preview (see the overall outlook) and then publish the page.

- Click on the **eye icon** ◉ located at the bottom left section of your Elementor dashboard.

- Once you are satisfied with the preview, select the **publish icon**  to publish your page.
- You can click on the "**have a look tab**" shown to have a look at the website.
- You can also save your content as draft by clicking on the arrow next to the **publish icon.**

How to Hide Post Title with Elementor In WordPress

- Navigate to your WordPress dashboard, click on **posts** and select a post from the list that has the title that you want to hide.
- Once the post has come up, tap on **edit with Elementor** and you will be redirected to the Elementor dashboard where you can edit the post with Elementor.
- Scroll down to the bottom of the **Elementor dashboard** at the left side of the screen and tap on the **document setting** icon.
- Under the **general setting,** scroll down and toggle the **hide title** box to **YES.**

About the Author

Konrad Christopher is a video software expert with several years of experience in videography and software development. He is consistent following the latest development in the Tech and software industries and has an eye for high-end video equipment and software. He loves solving problems and he's enthusiastic about the software market.

Konrad holds a Bachelor's and MSc degree in software engineering from Cornell University, Ithaca. He lives in New York, USA. He is happily married with a kid.

www.ingramcontent.com/pod-product-compliance
Lightning Source LLC
LaVergne TN
LVHW081530050326
832903LV00025B/1706